PRESIDENT OBAMA

&

The Principle of Continuous Improvement - Volume 2

Sifwat Ali

authorHOUSE®

AuthorHouse™
1663 Liberty Drive, Suite 200
Bloomington, IN 47403
www.authorhouse.com
Phone: 1-800-839-8640

First published by AuthorHouse   4/13/2009

ISBN: 978-1-4389-5687-9 (sc)
ISBN: 978-1-4389-5688-6 (hc)

Printed in the United States of America
Bloomington, Indiana

This book is printed on acid-free paper.

DEDICATION

Dedicated to the Founding Fathers
Especially
President Thomas Jefferson

ACKNOWLEDGEMENTS

I would like to acknowledge all my family members, in particular my son Kashif Ali, in the design of the front and back covers. I would also like to thank the design team at Authorhouse for several good suggestions during the design and production processes for this book.

CONTENTS

FOREWORD

A bird's eye-view of the difficulties facing the nation is first presented to the incoming Obama Administration and the new Congress. The specific problems are then described in some detail. Certain solutions, both from the current and futuristic perspective, are presented. An attempt has been made to keep the concepts and solutions explained in an understandable manner by mere mortals.

The book has ten chapters, eight of which deal with a specific area of difficulty, its explanation and solutions, presented from the perspective of an ordinary citizen who is neither a politician nor an economist. For example, the issue of infra-structure development is described in great detail. The sections deal with simply asking the "meaning of change in Washington" to suggesting that the infra-structure of the city of Washington has to change first. As long as people run in the elections against "Washington" in every other part of the country, they may get elected but as they enter Washington, the city will change *them*, before they change "Washington". Thus an infra-structure change is suggested for the city of Washington first, followed by other terrestrial (bridges, roads, veteran's hospitals etc.) and extra-terrestrial (ground satellite tracking sites and other space related) infra- structure projects to create millions of jobs in this sector alone. Each such chapter is then followed by a combination of real (and fictional?) desires on behalf of the ordinary citizens of this great country. For example, the chapter on infra-structure developments ends, after the problems and certain solutions, with the following:

One might seriously look to see, if there is enough capacity in our heads to expand the non-governmental population in Washington's midst while creating an exemplary infrastructure underground and above ground for generations to marvel at. A city that looks and feels like the head and the heart of a nation on a planet far away. Tear down some buildings that are hard to maintain and environmentally archaic. This is change that Obama and his generation could be remembered for. Is it possible to ignore the skeptics and start the change that will begin the works programs creating so many opportunities; a new space age shall dawn. The Earth will have traveled through the space, crisscrossing the heavens, and the only sky visible will be from the future.

I invite you to take a hard look at this book, dedicated and presented to the *nation* as a gift. I do want to thank my wife and children who encouraged me to do something concrete rather than merely pontificate and "Author-house Publishing" for doing their part speedily.

CHAPTER I
Election of a President

1.0 The Obama Fever

The idea of the second volume as a book came about from a poem I wrote back in July 2008 called Obama, in my mother tongue "Urdu", widely spoken in Northern India and Pakistan, when the then Senator Obama was not given any chance of getting the *nomination* of the Democratic Party let alone be elected president of the United States. I am a citizen of the United States, a Muslim, a registered Republican, and had never voted for a democrat, since Ronal Reagan. However, in listening to Obama, I felt something that I was unable to objectively put my fingers on; but it had a profound impact on the heart, as If the sixth sense had come alive. I presented the poem in two gatherings in August and September where it was applauded and well received. Then two days before the election in early November, I decided to record it in my voice and put it on the internet. The poem had certain references that I thought could hurt Obama and so I waited until the last minute, since I did not want even one vote to be affected or swayed by my poetry. Here is a non-poetic translation of the first part of that poem (think June 08).

Around the beacon[1] of Obama moths are swirling around
What is behind this madness? Only God knows!

---

1   In the first couplet the word "beacon" is the translation of a word called mish-al, a play the poet is making on the word, as in Urdu it sounds a bit like Mr. Obama's wife Michelle

We too are being warmed by its heat
We are afraid that in the mist of every one's
intoxication we too shall be intoxicated

There is some hope that the long chain of prejudice shall break
The principle of Oneness of Man, under
God's law, has started to excite me
The mental slavery has a new hope O Aibak[2]
If this becomes reality, we will write much fiction

Half the blood of the Muslim is good enough in the beginning[3]
We have been recognized by the "people of patience"

O Almighty, it is for your sake that we have started this journey
We are marching to let our Votes be
counted in the election of the President

O ye Sifwat[4] your eyes are reflective of the
Stars (i.e. you see the destiny pre-determined)
It is for this reason that we are madly attracted to Obama
The full poem which has three more couplets of the post election environ-
ment has been published in reputable magazines from India and Pakistan
and will not be presented here.

1.1 Predicting an Obama Victory

I was in fact predicting long before it was prudent that I
have read the stars and it is Obama who will become the
president among a plethora of candidates Republicans and Democrats. As
I read my poetry to the crowed, primarily to American's of Pakistani and
Indian descent but mostly Muslims, I realized that they were opposed to

---

2   The name "Aibak" (pronounced as A-e-buck) refers to the first Muslim
King of India who founded the **Slave Dynasty** in Delhi a thousand years ago.
This is a long story in itself – The point is that if Obama becomes the president
in reality and is even marginally successful, much fiction will be written, every
fable and every story a thousand or more years down the road

3   Mr. Obama is NOT a Muslim, because he says so. However, his father
was a Muslim the day he was born and the day he died and is buried as a Muslim. It is unclear to me if President's mother had ever accepted Islam – so at least
half the "blood"

4   The last Couplet has the name of the poet in Urdu tradition

Obama for his remarks about Pakistan, where he allegedly had threatened to "bomb" Pakistan. I realized that there was a bigger problem, as none of them wanted to hear his name, although they liked the couplets themselves as authentic poetry metered properly. That one comment from Senator Obama was "proof" that he was anti-Pakistan, even though Pakistan had been an ally of the US for the last sixty years (as opposed to India that was a Soviet ally until its breakup and even now gives more weight to Russia compared to the USA). My own preference was that we should all vote for Obama. So I called the owner of the leading newspaper in "Urdu" published from New York and sent him an article pleading to the folks of Pakistani origin to vote for Obama. The paper translated my article and published it as I wanted. Here is the gist of what I wrote:

"When I first landed at Philadelphia International airport, the city had barely recovered from the scars of the race riots in the late sixties. Young and very energetic then, I decided to take a tour of the eastern seacoast from Montreal in Canada to Miami. To my amazement the rural parts of the United States still had bathrooms separate for the blacks and the whites. The Churches were carefully segregated as well. Given the race relations, never in my wildest dreams I would have thought that a black person, a family man, highly educated attorney, will have a very good chance of becoming the president of this great country. I am a registered Republican, who has never voted for a democrat, before, will now vote for Mr. Barak Obama for the Presidency of the United States. Here are my reasons:

1. The most important reason in my mind is that it cuts all the barriers once and for all and someday my children or their children can dream of becoming the president of this country. That it is possible for the humanity in its entirety to dream big.
2. We have reached the next plateau in the perpetual struggles started by our Prophet that Oneness of Man must be preserved under God's law (just as the oneness of the Almighty is - Refer to "Islam *is* the future - A new Calendar for Humanity" by the author)
3. Mr. Obama has demonstrated steady leadership qualities in the last twenty months better than his opponents both in the Democratic Party as well as his opponents in the Republican Party.

For me this is one huge positive step for humanity. Mr. Obama has been able to articulate this greatness of Oneness of humanity without engaging in racial conflict and in fact staying above it. For me the greatness also comes from the fact (like me) that he has been raised essentially as an orphan. Having worked hard all his life and yet has found time to serve the cause of the poor and the oppressed. This is precisely the call of the day, not just in the United States, but the world over. I therefore recommend that we vote for Mr. Obama".

People, after reading the article, gave me feedback, and many of them changed their mind. One person confided that until he read my article, he was looking at the micro concern of Pakistan and not the larger issue of "Oneness of Man under God's law" and now had a higher calling. We have five votes in the family and the concern was raised. What if it turns out that he is just another corrupt politician from Chicago? I responded by saying that our votes are only as good as the information available to us. That is a weakness of the system called Democracy, where we are just numbers, the level of our piety is not counted. I asked my son, if he had given money towards this election, to which he said yes – twenty-five dollars for Obama. Did you, he asked and I nodded in affirmative and said – one hundred for the same candidate. In the end all five voting members voted for Obama. I am pretty sure that a similar discussion ensued among the members of every family that *thinks of tomorrow*. It didn't take long and all the pundits were in agreement on the election night. Obama was now the President-elect. We, the country, thus made history and now that it is reality, it is time to also write a bit of non-fiction in this treatise, may be even talk about the point of view of us oppressed Muslims.

1.2 The Change in the Thought Process

A complete change in political thought process was advocated by the incoming president. While we have a right to do so we are probably dreaming that any significant changes shall occur in the way Washington treats its own citizens or deals with a foreign government. The devil is in the detail, as they say. *But will it be too much to ask for the introduction of the concept of "Principle of Continuous Improvement" (PCI). The principle simply states that all things are going to perish, or cease to exist, unless improved in form and function. The Sun is decaying into a red giant and the roman numerals are not used in algebra. Although the more "axiomatic", the longer it will take to perish. It is true about anything in nature or manmade (the only exception might be in the definition of the Almighty). PCI is certainly true about democracy. Unless improved in form and function, democracy will perish in its current form as it has before in Roman and Greek times. There are no guarantees. A thorough explanation and definition are given in the first book.*

So what are those improvements that we can talk about without *jolting* the system? Jesus, for example, wanted to change the way the temple was being run in Jerusalem. Instead of using the temple to inculcate piety, the "lobbyists" were using it more as a market place with tables of money changers and animals to be sold and so on. So he proceeded to turn the tables and landed into a lot of trouble, jolting the system. God forbid, I am not looking for a jolt of the system, nor is Obama. But it might still be a long arduous struggle. A quick success requires mass approval, and we hope and pray that the people of the United Sates will be there with him for a just struggle to further elevate the consciousness of humanity. Obama's election means that masses have given their approval for a new paradigm. The change I am advocating therefore must be gradual, peaceful, and in accordance with PCI.

First on the domestic front, philosophically at least, recognize PCI and make sure that a change for the better is essential for posterity. Let this be debated throughout this nation and in congress and ask ourselves, is the Congress that tool that allows us to implement PCI. Are we willing to admit that some of the "principles" themselves may be subject to PCI? Let us start very slow. Can we simply beg that our labor laws be identical for all of humanity? Is it possible to move to implement that, as a starting point, just in Canada, the United States and Mexico? Can we simply require that the minimum wage in Mexico and Canada will not be less than the federal minimum wage in the United States? Can we come up with a schedule when this will be possible? What can the private enterprise do to help? Such a step will be an effort for us to make NAFTA fairer. The person who suffered in Ohio, whose job was "shifted" North or South is the individual to whom the society is responsible and the nation is answerable. That will be a good example for humanity, a beacon of light. It might take a decade, but Obama could point out something which he started and completed by the next president and so on. Is it possible to ultimately eliminate a terrible economic system and the labor in the US is treated just as fairly and unfairly as in Mexico and so on? This will have a profound impact on immigration and so on. If we could improve in form and function, this one issue, we could implement several corollaries to this complex theorem; where are you Newt Gingrich, come and help.

Second, in the global arena, and here I may be entering in the arena of fiction. It is estimated that there are 1.7 billion Christians and around 1.3 billion Muslims. Christianity is senior to Islam by about six-hundred years, hence the difference in the following. Clearly both religions are relatively speaking newer and popular. They are both fiercely competitive (in trying to win converts) and sometimes the followers cross the line at the populace and at the "government" levels. Together the followers of the two religions, however, account for roughly half the global population. If the followers of these two religions were to come closer, then by the theories of first "theology" and then "democracy" the oppression should be eliminated from the Earth. Also the economic well being of the poor of the Planet and beyond will be championed. If the two were to come together, it will eliminate unnecessary competition. It will eliminate exploitation. It will strengthen the basis of the law. There is a little hope from the Islamic side. However, articulating that is a real challenge given the climate. Let me try very briefly here while a formal argument will be given in Chapter IX - the Quran has extended the olive branch to the Christians from day one and says addressing the Muslims (V verse 82) "And thou will find the nearest of them in affection to those who believe to be those who say: Lo! We are Christians. That is because there are among them priests and monks and because they are not proud". The word proud is from the official translation referring to the humility, they, the priests and monks, feel in the service of the Almighty. The Jews should not despair, as I will be the first one to fight on their behalf, and alongside them, if another Hitler were to arise on the Christian scene. Can Obama address the real issues and bring the two sides together? Thus far he is respected by both sides. Again slow and steady hand is required and fear from inertia has to be overcome.

1.3 Economics and the Religions
I know that religion (theology) and *politics* are supposed to be separate by the "rules" of democracy and the secularists and the constitutionalists will come looking for me with their sharp tongues, so I will not debate that issue yet. But is it possible to learn something from

religion when it comes to economics as the religion, and their founders, especially the two mentioned above, are vehemently against exploitation. The problem is that PCI requires us to examine the economic systems as well. The current global economic system is based upon a supposition that not only you can sell anything, but even sell things you do not possess. Further, the cost of raising the capital is more of a function of a theoretical calculation based upon how much a product or a service can be exploited. If prostitution becomes legal (as in Nevada), the banks as well as the IRS are there looking for their share. If the poor are exploited by the "States" in the most regressive form of taxation, called the lottery, the money is used to pay the teachers' salaries – indirectly then gambling is the source of income of those who our children look up to and learn from. It has been narrated that a rich gentleman (and someone who believed in Prophet Mohammed) asked him (and I am paraphrasing) "O Prophet of God! Can I sell something that I have not yet purchased"? This, in the lingo of New York traders, was a question about "future's trading". The reply was an emphatic "No". The explanation being that you might become rich in doing so and a few like you, but the nation will in the long run (it might take decades) suffer as a consequence of this exploitation. Might I suggest that the current crisis is the result of greed and, unjust and unnecessary exploitation without any sense of PCI? Unless we improve this type of trading, it will ruin the nation. The most recent Wall Street crisis is clearly unacceptable. Must we ask another Jesus to physically turn the tables in the temple of New York? Can we attempt to end the exploitation without jolting the system? Therefore two chapters, one on economy and the other on religion are devoted.

Globalization on a massive scale is *not* being achieved on the basis of specific time tested laws and is illegitimate in the minds of those who are exploited. Globalization is being achieved for reasons of pure greed and more greed on the part of larger corporation. It has been the largest transfer of wealth from the United States to a handful of countries. It might have brought prosperity in the hands of some of those in other countries and a few billionaires may have emerged in these emerging economies. The ordinary citizen in the United States had been robbed for that to happen. Globalization appears to be moving uncontrolled and no consistent plans exists. The back offices of a large United States Corporation that provide corporate service are in South Asia, and the American people cannot even understand the logic of simple vernacular from those who are trying to communicate with someone who is in their sixties; A few weeks of training for those whose mother tongue is not English is insufficient. In fact in some corporation, the bonuses of the employees depends on how much IT work they can outsource; illegal in my mind. I am all for helping others to improve their economy but it cannot be done in the way it is being done now. I am afraid that a jolt in the system will result in unnecessary hardship for all.

One area that must be given a longer term look are the laws governing home purchasing, property taxation on the first home, foreclosures, and if any one were to listen to me, the size of the dwelling. The mortgage system is good in as far as homeownership is concerned but very bad that it in fact anticipates inflation, and not only the banks are being rewarded for a reasonable profit, the people are being exploited due to some abstract inflationary pressure. So a thirty years mortgage is paying the banks three or more times the price of the home over that same period. Similarly the towns and counties are continuously increasing the assessment based upon "market" condition and benefit from the exploitation, rather than be part of the solution to lowering inflation and oppression. Then there are people like Madoff who should be thoroughly investigated (not stopped) if a non-commercial building like a mansion is being built. The nation must make sure that it is coming from legitimate sources and common sense is not being substituted for a Ponzi scheme.

The current economic system is several hundred years old and must be re-looked. First, there must be a simple principle employed that the actuaries can use to determine a legitimate ceiling on "exploitation". No one is advocating communism or socialism – I am only interested in the preservation and improvement of a just but a free-enterprise system. Parts of our economy are just and may provide an example in the new calculus.

1.4 Energy Resources

A chapter on the world energy resources is devoted to change the thought process which has been talked about so much. A new triad system of solar/wind/wave has been proposed to be spread out in 10 mile by 24000 mile strip on the equator giving us energy forever. The issue of clean nuclear power has been raised; a method of safe disposition of nuclear waste is also proposed. Many of these ideas may sound like science fiction – to me they are not. Remember, Obama becoming president two years ago was also fiction. Other methodologies of energy production and conservation have also been discussed. The Obama team should get some really new ideas in this chapter on energy.

1.5 Healthcare

The health care system is so vast and its concepts are indeed so very difficult to comprehend for a mere mortal like me – but I do have a little experience in the field in a very limited sense. In general though, anyone can and should expect the "American Health Care System" to be the envy of the world and provide a leadership role on health issues in space exploration as well. At the moment, it has turned into a fiasco. Roughly a quarter of the population receives (and sometimes does not) its healthcare through some emergency room mechanism. The money ultimately comes from the taxpayer. The issue thus is the will of the congress and the executive. The baby boomers are soon headed to these emergency rooms and the politicians don't have a clue. The current Medicare system is a random set of processes and lacks an overall structure based upon the new requirements. Any plan to remedy the situation is mired in such complexity that it is easier to work on rocket science and actually build a spaceship to reach alpha-centaury. A step by step approach is suggested to "triage" and resolve for maximum return on taxpayer investment. I have concrete suggestions to the best of my abilities. Any improvement in the ideas will always be welcome. An entire chapter on the subject is offered for thoughtful consideration for the would-be in power Obama team.

1.6 Foreign Policy

One area where the president and the executive branch have far more responsibility and authority is in the arena of foreign policy. The United States was considered a sole "superpower" at the breakup of the Soviet Union. I personally disagree with that notion. It was a blip in historical terms and the United States has been losing grounds to other nations ever since. To be a "superpower" a country has to lead the nations of the world through example. And although it helps, it is not possible to lead simply by raw military or economic powers. The power of ideas, tolerance, and mercy are equally important – otherwise the country breaks up from within through some type of a jolt. The trick is to be the leader without getting bogged down in a "foreign" war. If globalization is a real phenomenon and there is no sinister design to transfer wealth from the US, the problem of wars becomes trickier. I recognize that one chapter (VIII) on foreign policy is not sufficient - others can jump in or add to the incomplete analysis. How will Mr. Obama get out of the two wars without talking about false honor and victory, shall be a huge challenge. A detailed look on one of the troubled spots and suggested solutions is examined. Some other spots are also discussed in less detail in Chapter VIII on foreign policy.

Having given a hopeful direction, I shall now proceed to describe in detail what needs to be done by President Obama (and the nation) to meet our expectations of this historic change so that it becomes more than a symbolic change, a change on which a thousand years down the road, writers may write fiction about, and the historians may understand how history is made not just written.

CHAPTER II
The Economy

2.0 A Few Words on the Priorities
The most pressing issue of our times in 2008-2009 is "economics". The trouble is so great that many experts have compared it to the great depression of the 1930's. Whether that is true or not depends on what statistical information you look at and how you spin it. From my point of view President Obama has to make sure that an order has to be established to fix the great problems of our time. *The priority in my mind is the following.*

1. Banking and the look alike
2. Fixing the Unemployment problem
3. The people – "fix it in the housing crisis"
4. The manufacturing crisis is similarly very large
5. Balancing Imports and Exports will go a long way
6. Flight of capital from the United States must be checked
7. Make sure the Dollar remains the preferred currency everywhere
8. Balance the Budget of the United States and pay off the existing debt
9. Invest in Infra-structure projects, education, healthcare, energy and political reforms
10. Get a buy-in from the folks to spend wisely in America, slow down the transfer of wealth

The items in number nine have to start now and in parallel. The reason it is number nine in my list, is because we want some mechanism to generate capital and not just borrow and print currency. A common sense discussion of the above problems is desirable as in the fog of the details, the big picture is lost often times and the solutions of the problems create more problems than the solutions. It is a little bit like the invention of a new drug. If the side effects are going to kill most of the patients, then the drug has to be modified or a new one has to be invented. So it is essential that we keep the big picture and the picture is that the United States has to move forward steadily and not take one step forward and two steps backward. Simply put, keep the Principle of Continuous Improvement in your thoughts before taking any action.

We begin by simply looking at the banking industry. Elsewhere in this book I have lamented that the current banking system is two hundred years old and needs to be looked at so it is relevant for the next two hundred years. The first thing is first though. We all want to make sure that a) the banks are sound under the current regulations and are following all the government regulations strictly and b) those institutions that look like banks (i.e. Lehman Brothers) no matter how small or big are being watched by someone who looks and acts like the government to make sure they will not cause the larger economic systems to collapse along with them. *Paramount is to look at the "Regulatory Structure".* The current regulatory structure has led to the most serious crisis, perhaps as great if not greater than the depression of the '30s. The government back then would not even think about printing so much currency without any checks and balances. Remember that the dollar was backed by gold back then, and therefore it acted as a constraint. Today all the theories of hedge funds have failed because in the end there is no hard constraint – just mathematical gimmicks and polynomials stretching to infinity and collapsing. The congress and President Obama must look at the fundamentals and overhaul the regulatory structure, otherwise the crisis will worsen. This does not however, in my humble opinion, means creating "credit safety" formulas managed by a Federal Agency. My issue is not so much of opposing the regulations. But that cannot be the only way of inculcating the Americans. It is they, who have to protect themselves, and no amount of baby-sitting will help; the overall environment will sicken the children.

My understanding is that as of the writing of this book (January 1, 2009), roughly $350 billion have been provided by the taxpayer to the banks and the look alike. Another $350 Billion is being readied for sick industries and so on. Now we are being told that another stimulus package is being readied for President Obama's signatures. Perhaps this is all essential and we applaud what is required. The danger is in its deep relationship to the value of the dollar and keeping the currency as the preferred currency of the world. The common sense part is very simple; if we have earned $100.00 but we owe $50.00 and our expenses are $200.00 we have several ways to solve it. If we are simply allowed to print another $150.00 we can resolve the problem, until the lender says the payment is not worth $50.00. You have diluted its value. So if we keep printing the currency or some such gimmick, the other countries of the planet are going to say that America is trying to pay us back with worthless dollars, it has become a paper tiger. Dollar will no longer be accepted. I am making it very simple but that is the net effect. So keep your stimulus in check and don't start spending what will end up being the drug that kills from side effects.

Let us talk common sense now about unemployment. This is the worst enemy after a failing banking industry. Once it gets to be higher than say 8-9 per cent, it is really bad news. A double-digit unemployment makes everything poisonous. In today's economy almost all the disputes, domestic and otherwise start with lack of money and employment. The chain reaction sets in and it results in an effective unemployment much higher than the government measurements. It ruins the civil part of the civil society. I am fearful that unless we can reverse the trend, we are already looking to reach an effective unemployment rate of depression era. The only way to get moving is for the Congress and the Obama administration to figure out a way of stopping the bickering in Washington and move fast. So if the auto industry is a genuine case, and I have no way of knowing it other than common sense, then it must be given time and money to recover, while appointing several watchdogs so taxpayer money is not stolen or falls victim to some insanity. The Federal Reserve must figure out a way to not dwell in monetary policy alone but look at the structural flow of the money into the economy so that its actions are felt in months and not in years. The structural flow of the Federal Reserve's policy to the common deserving businesses and persons should be given a "higher priority".

Once we have figured out reasonably that the banks and the look alike are "healthy", and we have taken care of the big but weak and sick guys, then there is a good chance we can begin to solve the housing crisis which some economists and pundits say is at the root of the current economic crisis. I disagree. The real major reason is a terrible monetary execution of the two foreign wars. We are where we are; and now what can we do to resolve the crisis? There are several ways to skin this cat but the banks have to operate within the strict new guidelines, whatever those are. The new guidelines should restrict the speculators from running hard to speculate in all sorts of fields, whether that is housing or oil prices or whatever. The housing depreciation has to be checked but not stopped. The burden of the lower housing prices has to be shared by the entire nation if the taxpayer is in the rescue business, including the banks. If the banks do not swallow their share, lower interest rates on healthy mortgages etc., eventually the chain reaction we have spoken about earlier will set in and no matter what stimulus, no one will be able to save the banks. The principle called PCI will take over.

Next a country with shrinking manufacturing base cannot continue to grow merely on the basis of regulatory overhaul of the banking system, monetary policy, service industry and consumerism. There is a crisis in the country now. It has partly to do with our noble desire to import cheap consumer products manufactured using cheap labor elsewhere. Like the proverbial ostrich we have buried our eyes in the ground while the entire world has been systematically attacking the US industry. This exploitation is at the root of the problem in our labor laws. This was less pronounced as higher technology products were exported in turn. But that has changed also. We are importing even the high technology components and labor. Further our dollar continues to become worthless as we turn more into a consumer and less and less a producer. Again this is common sense. Listen to the manufacturing industry without letting them produce lower quality products. What can be done to improve the base of the manufacturing industry? First, we should seriously think about taking steps to reverse the domestic corporations from re-locating overseas. Then once we have experimented a bit, encourage the underdeveloped parts of the country and poorer cities to look at their tax structures to attract a new class of cleaner manufacturing industries that will ultimately save the country from this shrinking muscle disease.

Balancing imports and exports is a major private sector challenge. Some guidance from the government(s) is required but this is an area where private industry has to realize that they have a duty to the employees in this country, and to the country itself, to keep research projects and lead in creativity and innovation. If the issue is only quarterly profit, the country is doomed to failure – and if that is the case, the political elite in and out of the government have to hold serious on-going discussions to avoid the ultimate decay without the slant of the lobbyists of a specific industry. Unless we can carefully balance the imports and exports, the country cannot remain a leader and ultimately the corporations will not be competitive (look at GM). If however, there are enough export dollars being earned, there is no harm in purchasing consumer products. Example: If Boeing exports enough aircraft to china, we can import all the safe toys from there. Certain key imports such as steel and so on require a deeper understanding of the problems. One area, where we have felt somewhat immoral is the import of human talent depriving other countries of their most important resource. There should no shame in this, only a balance, as we have a lot more talent right here as well. We must be able to control our borders but not become shy about legal immigration. If an Einstein, an Enrico Fermi or even a Sifwat Ali wants to legally immigrate to the United States, the country should welcome these fine gentlemen and any ladies like them – they add to the wealth wherever they go.

A related item is the flight of capital from the United States to other countries. This flight of capital is in a million different forms. I am not talking about a legal immigrant who is feeding his family back in civil war ravaged Congo to be restricted in sending a few dollars less. But if we look at NAFTA, it has systematically poured capital in Mexico which has either offset capital improvements in the plants here in the US or simply shut them off. The list of the countries goes on and on. The point is that the return on investment that we are deprived off as a result of the non-investment has a huge negative impact on everything. It then is further exacerbated by our government's generosity in reducing the import duty on goods coming from the plants overseas we erected to begin with. We now deprive the exchequer of the United States in not imposing a reasonable import duty to discourage the US corporations from excessive greed. Further, the profits can be moved outside of the country, and all that is left for the US citizen (like a drug addict) is to simply bankroll cheap imports. I am advocating a balancing act not a ban.

Let us talk about the almighty dollar that is about to become un-almighty unless we find wisdom. The Dollar is not backed by any universal metal, such as gold or hard assets in any significant percentage. What makes the dollar as good as gold is a little bit of jawboning, but at least on paper it is the United States GDP. So the world has a confidence factor in investing in the US dollar, its securities, IOU's and whatever else the jargon is. What has been decided so far is a conscious effort to devalue the dollar by our government. There are some who argue that a weak dollar is good for exports. If we are able to balance so that imports are in arrears, we can think of exports going up as a good thing. It used to be true that the United States exported large ticket items (aircraft etc.). But stupidity got in the way to the point of imbalance that the dollar has to be reduced in value to export US products.

Mr. Obama comes in with a budget deficit, so large the equations cannot be fathomed by physicists and the total Debt on the taxpayer of the United States has so many zeroes that mathematician cannot count them. In our history the debt has climbed more than the total GDP for the year, but the complexity was manageable. Currently it is at 70 percent? But we cannot despair – the country has faced depression before and we do have "hope", Obama's hope. The trick is to inject whatever dollars have to be injected quickly and arrive at the point from where steadily, even if at the pace of a tortoise, move to a balanced budget. It will perhaps take several years just to get to a point of significantly reducing the deficit. However, the effort has to be made from day one. The longer it takes to balance the budget, the larger the total size of the debt will be and the longer will it take to pay off that debt. We have to give ourselves a schedule to pay the debt off, a well calculated schedule. When we go to get a mortgage, we are told to pay it off in thirty years or whatever. Then we come along and say we have additional equity in the house and refinance a higher number for a different period, even a scheme called "reverse mortgage". The game is played until we are either too old and move to a nursing home or simply dead. I am very sad that our government has been doing the same as I do. If the government will do the same, then I wish I could just print the currency as well.

President Obama & The Principle of Continuous Improvement

I have an entire chapter on Infra-Structure development. The most important idea in that chapter is to change Washington D.C. by changing its
demographics. Make the city so that all the government functionaries and
their dependents (dependent on government spenders and not just their
families) become a minority and the city actually begins to look more like
the rest of the country than its current demographics - please see Chapter
IV. Similarly additional chapters have been written on Education (chapter
III), Healthcare (chapter VI), Energy (Chapter V), and Political Reform
(Chapter VII). Each chapter offers significant and perhaps new ideas. The
reason for adding these subjects to a separate chapter is the priority the
author places - for the Obama team to look at.

Lastly, here we request the people of the United States to conserve and
no matter what you hear from the advertisers and the like, add to your
savings, cut down your credit card debt, and reduce your shopping trips.
I will not ask the women to have just two pairs of clothes. You wash one
and wear the other. That will be too much for the economy to absorb. But
I will request from you to be quality conscious and keep in mind that the
product should be preferably (not necessarily) made in this great country.

2.1 The Third Rail of Socio-Political-Economics – Social Secu-
rity and Medicare

I will simply write two precise sentences on these "problems",
called Social Security and Medicare. These two programs, jointly speaking,
are a political football, which has been kicked so much that it does not look
like a football anymore – it will soon be obliterated and nothing will be
left to kick – FIX it. *IF the Obama team and the new Congress do not fix these
issues, they have already failed, regardless of what they solve on all the fronts
combined. Vice President Joe Biden, whom I am convinced, is the right person,
should take this bull by the horn and run.*

*We have given a bird's eye view and are looking for a speedy recovery of the
economy – The nation is counting on you O members of the Obama Team. We
know that you can be successful – I have asked the stars, and they are willing
to line up, but are looking for more precise coordinates and better calculations
of the trajectories from the nation.*

CHAPTER III
The Educational System

3.0 Fundamentals of Education

The current system of education is not as bad as some would like us to believe. However there are no goals of excellence that will take us to the next century (starting with 2009) and still be ahead in the crowd. The fact is that humans are one species and their brains are similarly highly evolved. There is nothing the United States can do that will not be copy-able or improve-able (from its definition) within fifty years regardless of the geography (we are not talking about Amazon jungle exceptions but Brazil as a nation will catch up in a few years). So the difference that keeps a leader in the crowd has to be always in short terms, like the runners in seconds. A country with highly advanced civilian research program can catch up in war games quickly and vice versa. The current system of starting with kindergarten and getting to grade twelve completely paid by the taxpayer appears to be fair. It does need to significantly improve though or it is headed as anything else towards extinction. I will come back to the improvements in a section later.

Next, the college education requires a lot more "attraction" much like the gravity itself. It has to be so naturally attractive that a child cannot wait to get going to a college, so much so that it becomes a childhood fancy. Not going to the college should be an exception, much the same way that not achieving a 5th grade education level is an exception. College education in the United States is not a "requirement"; it should be. The grades that should be classified as "not required" should be research subjects and certain higher professional formal certificates. A college to the level of sixteen grades should be a firm requirement from the industry, and from the government (they will call me a bigot, but if I could I will make it a voting requirement properly planned and scheduled). Another area under real stress is trade schools and higher level specialization. This is one of the major factors that quality and craftsmanship are in short supply – a requirement if we have to set spacecraft assembly lines – see chapter on infra-structure. There are all kinds of certifications but what is learned is miniscule in my mind. This has to change as well.

3.1 Education up to Grade 12

This is obviously the most fundamental area where everyone would like to see be of the highest quality. I am very much against all of these voucher and other "no child left behind" schemes. Any time one begins to make exceptions in these types of endeavors, it is to have accepted failure and the only option is to punish someone. Even "no child left behind" is akin to, weak and the old, in a caravan in the desert. They have to be especially cared for. To claim that a child needs to be rounded up so he/she is not left behind is absurd. The real problem is that mass producing educated children requires a robotic precision and the brains of Einstein(s) embedded in each school. Fortunately, there is a way. It is called the "Principle of Continuous Improvement" as we have discussed before. The current system has to be appreciably improved in form and function or else it will produce "illiterates". The function here is the "education" and the form is the precise ideology, evolutionary intellectual and mechanical processes which detail implementation. Put mathematically:

$$\Delta \text{ Education (time, Education Level, other terms) } / \Delta \text{ time}$$

This has to be measured. Note that time is factored to make sure that a change is measurable between two groups one practicing the new improved "form and function" and the other not.

The issue is significantly complex and must be phrased very simply by saying that when the team proposes to improve the system, it cannot be just words but required verifiable data. The verifiable data cannot be 2% or 10% improvement but a *continuous improvement*. If the formula itself breaks down, invent one that works. Let us go into a little detail to make the point more clear. The current mechanism in many States to fund the school system is based upon property taxes. As long as you own property (even if you have no children or your children have grown up, you still pay taxes in the system) you are then burdened by this additional tax. So the taxpayer is paying for the school system in one or the other form. This is highly inefficient on a national basis. The poorer the neighborhood, the poorer are the school systems. Further, the cities are bloated with such inefficient service's structure that their school systems are always under duress (economically). I think that in order to compete universally, one has to rethink the current system. Those who are extremely rich can send their kids to a very rich institution but they will and should learn *the same vernacular* sitting on mahogany chairs and better painted ceilings. Going into further details, teaching of the English language (or for that matter Physics) has to see a paradigm shift. To begin with one cannot have a classical (let us say) one hour session with students running away from the scene when the most important part of the lesson is being taught; *the solution is that the concentration levels of the children must improve. What can medical research do (without drugs) regarding concentration levels? This is not science fiction. Perhaps the session time goes from one hour to half hour but the concentration level goes from "one time" to "five times". If that is possible, you have just increased the number of subjects being taught from five to ten and so on.*

There are two other quick things I would like to point out. Education up to grade twelve has almost no relevance to "practical living". In almost all cases, the young man/woman coming out has more training on the nature of things simply by mixing among the youth; they can impregnate and give birth to babies, but nothing useful to an employer. This should be looked at by the local officials who have just as much at stake and not just the Obama team. Secondly, the respect of the teacher has to go up exponentially – a nation that does not respect its teachers will never learn anything. A rigorous course teaching the basics must be taught religiously before anything and must be repeated in every grade.

3.2 College Education

If we want to compete globally while going forward and have any chance of leadership in the world community, the college education up to full graduation (grade sixteen) has to be made FREE. I wish that all education could be advocated to be free but "intellectuals" may laugh at me, and at the nobility of my thought process as impractical. The first thing that occurs in accepting a fact of mental illness is the denial of the facts. One of those denials that have gone on in society forever is the importance of college education. We must accept the notion that college education is no longer a luxury, it is as fundamental as learning the courses in the fifth grade. The basic reason is that the amount of knowledge has increased so much that a simple twelfth grade education is inadequate. We are no longer living in a society where building a mausoleum called pyramid(s) is the end of our horizon. Now if the brain can be trained to absorb concepts at five times the speed, maybe we will not need college education for a few years. The easiest thing to do now is to work the numbers and find out what would it take to make the college education free. If Obama team will not find time to know the numbers to do it, I will. If we refer back to PCI, we may take the journey of free college education by simply taking one or two subjects first. To keep costs down, maybe we can make graduating in Physics free in the beginning, then Physical Chemistry and Mathematics and so on. Clearly, this can be sustained for a couple of years, as we do not want unemployed physicists driving taxis – although they will do it with caution and precision. More importantly, the other subjects are equally important.

Some of the same paradigm shifts are required in college level teaching as discussed above and must follow PCI. The learning institutions have certain responsibilities as well – it is not all government. The colleges and universities must look at the whole concept of tenure. While professors should be able to keep their jobs as long as they want, teaching and research must be balanced. My personal observation is that once professors are tenured, they work on what they want to work on which may be good for them; it is not necessarily good for the students. Also, this mad rush to publish or perish kills the students more than the professors. The real challenge is to have so many students and vacancies for teachers and professors (in the entire country) that there is no need for tenure. Finally a word or two on University reforms are in order. The universities of today are far more institutions of politics and intrigue (who gets the tenure and who is bringing more money and grants and so on) than great institutions of learning for scholarship a hundred years ago. Clearly for the Obama team, this part of the reform will not be the highest on the priority list – sadly though.

3.3 Religious Education

Traditionally religious education has been under the jurisdiction of the private religious schools and a voluntary phenomenon in general. However, there are schools run by various religious institutions but provide education with a curriculum as in the public school system. This is very good and should be encouraged with proper guidelines. I will propose at the risk of being incoherent that a national agency (the members need not be government servants) be established that encourages interfaith dialog. And in those religious schools that encourage this dialog grants should be given by this agency to foster religious understanding and tolerance at the very early age. If sex education can become a requirement primarily because it is a health issue, we can request similar understanding in the name of reducing wars and murder and promoting civility. Civility is the basis for a lasting democracy. We should thus use the PCI to enhance the peaceful conditions on the planet as it, in the end, will determine whether or not we self-destruct.

We end this chapter by quoting "Read: in the name of thy Lord who created. Created man from a clot...Who taught by the pen". We expect the Obama team to read in the name their Lord and always be sure that when there was complete darkness (ignorance), the Almighty said, let there be light, and ignorance turned into knowledge and wisdom which gave us the ability to see far in the future. It is this ability that is now required to fix the educational system and all that is darkness in the country.

CHAPTER IV
The Infra-Structure

4.0 The Meanings of Change in Washington

The first thing that comes to my mind is that Washington is primarily a town inhabited by the government functionaries, both civilian and military, their dependents, lobbyists, and anyone else that needs anything from the government or directly and indirectly works for these functionaries of Washington. Besides the "government" there are a few people who also inhabit the city who are collectively ignored as they are poor and not well educated. These poor people are constantly looked down upon. The next generation is just as non-productive as the first one. *If I were to exaggerate a bit, the folks of this minority in Washington can be described as:*

The huts, the slums, the shanty towns, everywhere abound
Words, grammar, vernacular, and different every sound
This is a cosmos by itself and the stars rather dim
The Sun is blanketed in the dust and the faces very grim
The roaming gangs, justice swift, eye for an eye
The needles, very potent, and everyone is high
Unreadable, garbled, graffiti on the wall
Illiterate, and indecent, still, children almost all
Plenty rock, plenty rap, cluttered nonsense trash
Dancing around in a circle, unproductive thrash
Misdirected talent plenty, ugly and abhorrent

May be a diamond in the rough, beauty not apparent
Reading, writing, arithmetic, here, there, or none
Sports uncivil in some places, and a lot of fun
Physics, math, hard sciences, and rusty every brain
Sharpening these thick dumb skulls futile strain
Race, color, and discrimination mantra every day
Fornication, prostitution, the unwed mothers play
The volunteers have disappeared and the politicians gone
The speeches given, the photos taken, news on and on

If the above picture of non-governmental Washington has to change, it must change its demographic picture. I know that a lot of countries have followed this model, and built capitals (Brasilia, Islamabad etc.) which have essentially also become towns like Washington (primarily government based) devoid of the feelings in the country at large. In some cases, the poor have been entirely excluded by making it impossible for them to live there. This perception must change. If I could, I will change the capital to be more accommodating. I do not wish to name cities like New York, Los Angeles or Chicago as I do not wish to create a gigantic metropolis. The idea is that in the capital city, the government has to become a small minority so that it can see how the "country" lives and feels. The Process of continuous Improvement (PCI) requires of us to change the current model, otherwise it will slowly perish or become extinct. People will run "against" Washington but will be unable to change it, leading to a sudden jolt which thoughtful people do not want.

You might sincerely differ on changing the demographics of the city of Washington. The reasons that originally lead to the creation of the Capital may well have been all good at the time. Two hundred years ago, the folks living in Washington were the only ones who paid any taxes to the Federal Government and the States wanted to be fiercely independent and not pay a dime to the "federal institutions". There may have been actual shootings among the States to preserve certain boundaries. There may have been a thought that the mingling of ordinary folk with high government officials will lead to more corruption. All these are issues of history and PCI has reversed them or the communications and technology improvements have made these issues archaic. So it makes sense to take steps to change the demographics of Washington and do it now.

I will suggest an approach roughly inverse to what is being practiced today. The city government should go to congress with Mr. Obama's blessings and declare federal capital to be tax exempt (the inverse of paying tax to the federal government two hundred years ago by the residents of the city).

1. The property taxes should also be abolished and the city be given the equivalent funds from congressional budget provided the living quarters are in multi-story buildings of more than ten stories – condos for non-welfare recipients. This will increase city population simultaneously conserving land. We will not discuss folks on welfare as what is about to be proposed will essentially eliminate the need.
2. The action above will be taken in such a way that the "public school system" becomes the envy of the world. Congress should again fund this. Washington should become the research center of the world. Goddard Space Flight Center may become the focal point, turning it into an academy of teacher's training for the future. Children should be medically, psychologically and physically examined if they have a learning disability. The learning disability should be understood for the benefit of humanity, and not to look down on the child. Similarly a child far more advanced than his peers be examined and understood again for the benefit of humanity.
3. The definition of "small business" can be improved and their taxes abolished, if they set up shop in the federal area.
4. Market forces must be "forcefully civilized" so that the city does not become a rich people only city. This is not to create utopia but inculcate fairness – remember that under PCI, utopia in not achievable.
5. People of all fifty states, ordinary people, must somehow be represented in state enclaves in far greater numbers based on their actual places of birth or any other fair criterion to take the places of lobbyists (a rotation of former selectmen, mayors, councilmen, ombudsmen, businessmen etc?). This, and in fact all the suggestions and concepts, need further discussions and thought. The idea is to create a microcosm of the entire country in the fairest way possible in a non-governmental sense.
6. Allow off-shore companies to relocate to Washington for pennies on the dollar.
7. Aggressively go after the criminals and clean up the city (a more merciful Singapore model?). Please see below a discussion on privacy issues.

4.1

The Infra-structure Talk and Millions of jobs
President Obama spoke of infra-structure development and
the creation of millions of jobs. Now what I am proposing
for Washington is the biggest infra-structure development project in the
history of the world. It is more ambitious than the building of the pyra-
mids.

Before I write anything else, a paragraph on the concept of privacy should
be looked at in some detail since this concept itself is subject to PCI. We
will not see the final chapter written during the Obama administration but
important milestones are achievable. Technology is making it impossible
to keep certain details of the daily life to remain private. We are hoping to
be a highly advanced society and do not and cannot all live in some remote
Himalayan cave. The more the interaction using more and more advanced
systems, the less likely it is to preserve aloofness. So what is important is
to *know and understand* that nothing is private (not event the private parts)
but who knows what has to be redefined and its purpose. The woman
wants to show her private parts to her doctor or to her husband but this
is not regarded as violations of privacy. Perhaps the government has the
data allowing it to know the precise picture of our private parts; the issue
is what is "suppressible" from the eyes of an oppressive government. Is it
possible to get alerted by a high technology system to make sure that alarm
bells are rung throughout the corridors of all the citizen's and government
houses that their government and its functionaries are up to no good?
Otherwise who truly cares that a doctor/rabbi/mullah knows that someone
was circumcised at age two weeks or whatever. The reason I have brought
this issue up-front is that it will be raised after the suggestions below and
the constitutional experts have to take it beyond experimentation.

First, to turn Washington around a team will draw 24th Century architecture of the new Washington, understanding the new demographics; the
population, the government, and the business centers and so on. The team
that will draw the architecture shall be the best possible on the planet
and represent the citizenry of the United States in all walks of life. This
architecture shall be debated and analyzed – but analysis shall not lead to
paralysis – and adherence to the schedules, project plans and the budgets
will be a patriotic duty. The architecture will start with a new paradigm in
which communication within the city and the rest of the world will not

be the only thought. The folks living in the capital of the world shall easily communicate with the family members who may be astronauts and their loved ones in the Space Stations, on the Moon, on Mars or wherever they may be.

The technology that the home is built on today is obsolete. The structural components that go in each home, each condominium every apartment are all archaic. It is a challenge to the scientists to build a house of 2500 square foot of livable space for less than ten thousand dollars that is structurally and environmentally sound and offers every modern necessity. This dwelling shall be fitted with a "super cable system" that is based upon the newest bit rates millions of times higher than the best today. The home of tomorrow has to become self sufficient.

Second, the architecture team shall propose to build underground/above ground "Fast Mobility System (FMS)" in Washington that becomes a model for humanity. You come down from your home on the 23rd floor on FMS and as soon as you start to leave the "home" you are moving to your desired location using a system that is envy of the best GPS systems in any entity from the fastest to the slowest moving aid to go from one location to the other within Washington. The system should be so good it will be copied by the rest of the country and the world with American know-how. The system will last and be improved over the next two to three hundred years. This "fast mobility system" will get rid of most of the road and subway technology from the nineteenth century. I do not wish to prejudice the engineers but a perpetual model similar to the seven layers of communications may be invoked or something even better.

Third, the architecture team will look at energy production. A complete chapter on energy production and *export* will follow. The talk of energy independence is defeatist. The thought process should be to increase energy production so that not only, the United States is self sufficient but actually exports vast amounts of electrical energy to the "rest of the world" at a penny per kilowatt, and we show below how.

The Washington project in itself will employ a large number of workers (my estimate is 1 million) for the next fifty years.

4.2

Terrestrial Infra-structure
A more comprehensive look at the projects would broadly divide them into two basic categories. First, those projects which are above ground, and second those which are underground. Examples in the first category might be roads and bridges. Examples in the second category might be water channels under Manhattan or any other large city. The current projects which the State Governors want are all worthy of a practical look and implementation if thought wise and prudent. Whatever is necessary in the short term is one thing but the infra-structure that keeps the United States a leader are not the ones being proposed by the Governors, at least in my understanding. They are of interim nature that will keep workers employed and keep the economy humming using money coming from the "stimulus packages" the current administration began and will be significantly augmented by the incoming Obama administration.

Most of us normally think that the infra-structure development means the building of new bridges, repairs of the existing ones and so on. It means building new roads, expanding current roads (say from two lanes to three lanes) and even repairing the pot holes. It should also mean creating a new vast mass transit system, which in America barely exists. This infra-structure is possible only in the context of the Fast Mobility System described above. It requires a new thought process and a new paradigm. A mass transit system is not possible until it can actually *outperform in safety, security, cost of operation, cost to the consumer, and make the use of automobile convenient only as an exception and significantly more expensive.* Again this requires a significant shift in the demographics requiring a different type of planning.

The infra-structure development that I am talking about will make the United States a leader in future in the fictional sense and also a reality in the field by example. It is not the interim projects the governors of the states want; some of which may be necessary to get us out of the current fix at the state levels. Here is what might be regarded as futuristic infra-structure development project. Think of the example of an old city like Boston, which for historical reasons grew as needed and even today is difficult to find your way around in. On the other hand moving around in Manhattan is relatively speaking somewhat simpler (arrangement of streets and avenues and numbering/naming conventions etc.). The country highway structure is similarly laid out a bit as a historical phenomenon and possibly based upon cost/benefit analysis suiting the population and commercial centers. Same is true for airports and so on. This is alright now but not futuristic. A futuristic as well as a practical system requires us to look at airport/road/railroad system as an integrated system. It fits the concept of FMS in which a person's *actual travel is the least inconvenient part of the journey*. Historically (two hundred years ago or more) we have thought of a journey of a few hundred miles as treacherous and unpredictable in which loss of life and property was very much a possibility. A true friend was one with whom you had travelled and found in him qualities you would admire after the journey. While we have come a long way, a journey of even fifty miles remains a hardship. Traffic jams, and accidents, on rare occasions even road rage and shootings are very much part of the daily commute.

The new infra-structure is thus a highly intelligent system which can *anticipate* a person's travel, and make it almost as convenient as moving around in his/her home – food, bathrooms, wheelchair access, ambulances, fire and police are all there or anticipated without impediment. Can I hint on a specific project, which I would like to be taken up? Can we have a No-speed-limit highway, four lanes each way between Miami and Seattle Washington in which two out of eight lanes are for a rapid railroad and an airport every four hundred miles along the road? This is like going along the hypotenuse of a rectangle triangle. There are other things I can suggest as part of this project from the FMS concept but you get the idea.

Another area that has remained neglected in a big way is our ability to create under-water infra-structure for our benefit and preparing us for exploration beyond the planet. We are not simply talking about the underwater telephone and other cables. A specific mega project that will transform the world is discussed in Chapter V on energy independence. It will create millions of jobs the world over. This is an example of globalization where the United States can be a leader but it does not have all the disadvantages of net out flow of wealth by trillions of dollars. Beyond this specific mega project, the technology of under-water exploration and lack of any permanent deep under-water research station is sad. Not even the fables of Atlantis have been able to excite and entice us.

Let me "fictionalize" one other aspect of "creating" jobs before the next section. I wish it can be treated as a real issue. It is this: creating jobs is only fifty percent of this infra-structure development the other is inculcating "work ethics". I am sorry to lament that while worker's rights have continued to increase and that is a good thing. However, the pride in one's workmanship has deteriorated in my humble opinion. The knowledge of the worker, along with a meticulous attention to detail is not emphasized equally. The United States is not going to continue to be a leader if the workers available are less industrious and more expensive and the employer is forced to look at the immigrant labor or needs to go abroad just to get the work ethic. I am sorry to lament that too much old money and no work ethic is a sure sign of decay and destruction. Therefore I shall mandate "work ethic" training for each new employee and continual repetition as often as possible. In fact, if I was a vicegerent of the prophet(s), I will mandate it five times a day – but I am not, so it will have to be determined by the human resource person(s) and other considerations.

4.3 The Extra-terrestrial Infra-structure

So far I have discussed a mega project on and about Washington itself, and other projects elsewhere but pretty much stayed on the Earth. There is so much to do and not enough time to write. I feel like taking a shovel and starting right now. However, there are vast opportunities that can create ten times as many jobs as on the Earth, if we were to create an infra-structure on the planet (and then go beyond) that is primarily about looking for resources to serve the humanity beyond the planet Earth. Let the humanity face the facts. Either we will stay on this planet and be essentially "hunters and gatherers" and perish, like the dinosaurs, based upon the PCI, or fulfill the ultimate dream of spreading throughout the cosmos and the heavens, again based upon the same PCI, the choice is ours. Now Mr. Obama can just be a better president than Mr. Bush or he can resume where Kennedy left off – beyond the planet and lead humanity into a different yet promising direction.

Now the Earth Stations to track satellites, the space shuttle, the space stations(s), even a colony on the Moon while constituting the first stages and the building blocks of this infra-structure, they are not quite extraterrestrial in nature as all these (including the Moon) are actually satellites of the Earth. Part of the reasoning for development of the FMS structure is to learn to "crawl" before we can actually learn to walk on a planet other than the planet Earth; the first goal might be to set foot on (for example) Mars. To simply go to the Moon or even Mars and then return means nothing to me. This has to be more than travel, it has to be a journey for humanity where we will proclaim something, create something, where a new plateau of self-awareness shall be reached.

Let us discuss a not so out of the box idea that can open up a million jobs in its own right. Remember Henry Ford, the gentleman who set up the assembly line to build the Model-T. The idea of today should be to set up an assembly line for the design and manufacturing of space ships. Let the Chinese supply toys and more toys. It will be a thing of American leadership to set up a plant that will create, design, and manufacture a five seat space craft that can take a family to a bunch of space stations for a day or two. This will create a sense among the people of the world that they are fighting over nothing. It will create a sense that our destiny is to explore beyond the planets in the solar system. It will help set new standards of measurement of universal time. It will help open the stock market in Tokyo and New York at the same time. The Obama leadership may not be able to achieve all of this but at least set the direction rather than internal fighting on the planet.

Let us set up three large space stations between the Earth and the Moon moving around the Earth in such a way that they are roughly one hundred thousand kilometers (sixty thousand miles) apart. Let them be visible along with the moon or whatever geometry most appropriate. The distances can thus be shrunk and one can reach/hop using the space craft in about five hours (same as going from New York to Los Angles) from the Earth to the nearest one of these space stations and then hop to the next. Like the rest areas along the highway, they can supply food and shelter – the tricky part will be to make sure that the toilets work as well. The point is that we have to open up an industry that really explores the possibility of "long" distance exploration. If there are enough hopping stations, we will expand the industry and create a lot more jobs on the assembly line and excitement than ever before. Clearly thoughtful planning is required to acquire and conserve energy, water, and food resources while not putting an additional burden on the Earth and its environment. Further down the road, conservation of mass and energy will be big issues as well. Again what I have wished here will not be achieved by the next administration but it is capable of creating a lot more jobs and to keep America as the strongest leader of all times. If it only achieves five percent in the area of extra-terrestrial infra-structure, it is already a step forward.

A number of mega projects have been discussed and proposed. These projects, if commenced with wisdom, are able to create more good paying jobs than available qualified work force. If someone has better ideas they should propose new projects or correct me. The challenge is in doing things. None of these projects will get off the ground unless we have our priorities carefully sorted. An enormous amount of money is being spent in unproductive wars across the globe (please refer to the chapter on foreign policy suggestions). We summarize this chapter:

One might seriously look to see, if there is enough capacity in our heads to expand the non-governmental population in Washington's midst while creating an exemplary infrastructure underground and above ground for generations to marvel at. A city that looks and feels like the head and the heart of a nation on a planet far away. Tear down some buildings that are hard to maintain and environmentally archaic. This is change that Obama and his generation could be remembered for. Is it possible to ignore the skeptics and start the change that will begin the works programs creating so many opportunities; a new space age shall dawn. The Earth will have traveled through the space, crisscrossing the heavens, and the only sky visible will be from the future.

CHAPTER V
Energy Resources

5.0 What is the Importance of Energy?
I am sorry to begin by saying that the importance of energy is really not understood by the politicians or the folks at large. Almost all of the modern day politicians have never discovered or engineered anything complicated. The scientific understanding of most people of energy has also been evolving as is the case with most scientific knowledge. Unfortunately it has taken gas crisis and Ozone layer issues for politicians to even acknowledge that there is a political problem. Only a few hundred years ago, the world had no formal plans to produce more energy – it was not a political issue. People produced lamps and chandeliers running on a gamut of "natural" fuels. They borrowed "fire" from the neighbors next door to cook. Temples kept fires burning on a continuous basis. The biggest source of warmth and crop production was (and still is) the Sun which aided human beings gain energy mostly through food. Today, most people talk about energy as fuel producing power resulting in the mechanical motions of their cars. They see energy in the form of electricity, used for all sorts of tasks. They see energy in the form of what comes out of oil and gas furnaces - heating their houses. They see water rushing down a channel annihilating whatever is in its path.

In practical terms, for most people, energy is something that is used by them without fear of ever running out; rarely are they afraid that there will be political trouble. For others the fossil fuels as a huge source of energy, burning non-stop, and raising the global temperature enough to reduce crop yield, endanger biological life as we know it and so on are huge political and moral issues. They know that giant corporations are busy producing this substance called energy, anyway they can, and transporting it across the globe. Those among us who call themselves environmentalists are appalled at our lack of respect and unimpeded burning away of the resources of the planet; they would like to jolt the system to the point that goes beyond the heated debates. Clearly it is time to act.

In my humble opinion, the producers, the consumers, and the environmentalist are not doing the best they can. It is a relationship that needs to be improved and perhaps regulated. First of all, we must figure out through specific definitions and laws of setting up infra-structures to produce energy that is based upon environmentally sound principles. Next, we must find creative ways to produce energy, billions of times more than we do now. Finally, it is essential for humanity at large to be absolutely frugal about consumption. It is one resource on the planet we cannot burn away as we require it here and in explorations beyond the planet. It should be noted that any exploitation of energy which is being used to run an appliance, a car move, a train in motion, anything with mechanical movement, will generate some heat, as there is no engine whose efficiency is one. But to produce and use fossil fuels to enhance greed and cause enormous climatic changes has to be slowed down and ultimately stopped. It might take several decades but a steady and measureable progress is required.

In an article I wrote roughly ten years ago, referring to global warming, I pointed out that we should now look to a policy of adaptation. In other words, even if all the countries as a result of some treaty, and enhancements to that treaty, got together and implemented all the recommended safeguards, it will still take a hundred years or longer to effectively eradicate damages caused by emissions of carbon dioxide which tends to naturally linger on in the atmosphere. We should hasten the required research to see how we can produce seeds and plants, which will be heat resistant, and yield levels, will not drop. Also, due to the possibility of floods, and rise of the ocean levels additional problems are expected. We already know that harbors on world scale "below" the sea level, will be affected by any significant rise in the ocean levels. In infra-structure development one has to seriously think of dykes etc. In addition, various river deltas need to be carefully studied to see what other possibilities exist. There might be some good news as well, in that several new small ports might become feasible. Also, the river deltas that have become puddles of water (Colorado?) may provide fertile ground for the food chain and the echo system in general.

I am sorry to say that a decade long program that Obama and the team have talked about – a Manhattan type project or a Man on the Moon type program *will not be enough to achieve energy "independence"*. We will arrive at a real change only with a different thought process. Even the energy required to fulfill our modest dream of demographic changes in the city of Washington is not available with the nineteenth and twentieth century thinking. The problem is not that we do not have enough resources for the next several hundred years; the problem is that our thought process is too limited. Sure there are environmental issues but we cannot clear our future path through the forest merely hacking through conservation. That will be against PCI leading to human devolution.

5.1 A Solar Panel Ring on the Equator – building a Triad Electrical System above the Ocean

Can a star be harnessed by humans much like an atom has been? Are we really God's vicegerent or is it just fiction? Have we been thinking too small? Clearly this has to be understood and thought through. I am certain that by using the "Principle of Continuous Improvements" we have work to do. The energy production is thus one of the biggest issues of our time and shall remain forever. So where will the energy come from (not the small amount we produce worldwide today) but to take the current production and multiply it by a billion times and more? It has to come from natural sources of energy such as the stars (or planetary surfaces that produce vast amounts of energy and are essentially uninhabitable or such combinations as are possible to explore.

My humble suggestion would be to build a single 10 miles wide by 24000 miles "long" (around and along the equator?) triad of solar panel, wind, and wave panel apparatus, around the earth mostly on the ocean (It may be better to build two five mile rings at 30 degree parallel for scientific reasons but the one on the equator will be less politically volatile). The solar panel(s) and the triad ring around the Earth will produce vast amounts of energy to be distributed by a "global grid". It does not require the use of any fossil fuels. Please also note that

I am not advocating building the electrical grid touching the water surface. It is significantly complicated but *the technology is there to do it now in such a way that no harm shall come to the wild life or environment as we begin to harness wind, and ocean wave energy while erecting solar panels. I call it the triad system.* This global grid will attract the attention of the nations not so advanced and might even be willing to take part in the project through UN loans or some creative financing mechanism. If there is technology of distribution unknown, we should find out how. This will reassert American leadership the way it should be reasserted. A formal description of this project is in my last book. The United States can experiment along a tiny length just a few miles from the coast for feasibility.

5.2 Nuclear Power

Next I wish to talk about safe and environmentally sound Nuclear Power generation. The first and the foremost and possibly the most controversial concepts in this arena are the safe storage of the highly radioactive waste product(s). I will suggest two ideas in this regard. Uranium is found in nature in rocks etc. The centrifuge process and other processes are used to purify it at different concentration levels for different uses in the industry. Similarly Plutonium is also widely used in the nuclear industry. There is radioactive waste and by-products that may also be highly radioactive after useful life in a reactor or in a nuclear "battery". The safest way to dispose it is to let this be transported and gently dropped to the uninhabitable planet Mercury in a non-reusable cheap rocket produced in the assembly line discussed previously. Mercury receives unimpeded radioactivity from the Sun larger than that coming out of the waste products - so much radio activity and lack of atmosphere, it will be in essence "safe storage". If someone has an objection, it can be sent to the Sun directly never to affect anything. It is clearly a problem in as far as storage on the planet is concerned. All nuclear materiel producing countries must join the effort and contribute to the storage of radioactive waste on Mercury etc.

After solving the above problem, next, take the current nuclear power plants sites and increase their capacity ten times or hundred times or whatever – just start over and build much higher capacity plants. If we just started doing that, it should create far less additional environmental problems as the new technology is hopefully more advanced and sound from that perspective than the current one. There is always the syndrome of "not in my back yard". That problem is solved as well by staying put. There will be additional concerns, but those can be resolved working with scientists who also care for the environment. Specific goals may be set of supplying us with one hundred kilowatts at one-thousandth of the current cost.

5.3 Coal as a Source of energy

We cannot abruptly stop the use of any form of matter, liquid or gas from producing energy. What can be a requirement, for example, are emissions from any of the forms over a scheduled time frame. The environment cannot be repaired by turning off a single form of usage and lay off a mass of people resulting in political chaos. However, PCI requires a level of research that we have abandoned. Take a look at the history of understanding temperature scales. What did it take to reach as close to absolute zero as the Uncertainty Principle would allow. Coal is a source for producing warmth and electricity. Can we liquefy it and process it like we clean oil. If that technology does not exist, and the alternative sources are more efficient, the people must be re-trained by the government from the educational funds (not derived from lottery). The United States is blessed with coal resources and therefore merely keeping it in the ground is hard to swallow, but we should be able to wait a few years and wait for the right technology.

5.4 Hydro Electric, Wind and Other Ideas

Now, there are folks that have other ideas. Those include enhancing the continental grid to take advantage of the "wind corridors" on land, natural gas exploration, even environmentally sound drilling for oil; none of these however, are enough to meet the long term energy requirements of the country. If energy becomes too expensive (we just had a taste of it in the form of gasoline prices) it will hamper the growth of the country, its leadership position in the world and seriously impede the country's development. All of these ideas have some problems associated with them. Take the case of Hydro-Electric Power which we had always thought of clean and renewable source of electrical power. Not anymore. We have been told that building dams is bad for the life forms; it destroys the echo system. We have been told that countries downstream lose their share of water. We have been told that huge artificial lakes created above the dams deposit too much sediment and in the end (fifty or hundred years) the system becomes useless unless significantly improved at great costs. Let us take the case of wind corridors; we are afraid that without modeling it completely and understanding all of the ramifications we may be looking at micro-level climate change. Think of it this way, if a mountain is erected in the path of rising clouds from the oceans, the clouds rise and become cold and might rain before nature intended for them to rain. The amount of rainfall far beyond the mountain range is then affected. I am not saying that we should stop at second order perturbations, if that is what it is; it is better to investigate and get the environmental specialist along with you rather than constantly fight them.

5.5 Conserving Energy and the Duties of Environmentalists Conserving energy has risen to the third most important object necessary for human development. Air, water, and Energy give us a new slogan "AWE". This can never replace the three C's but it comes pretty close. We are in awe of these resources. Our life depends on them. We no longer live in the desert or close-by civilizations anymore. As part of the new home design argued earlier, conservation should be a paramount concern. Human presence in the home should trigger a number of responses from the new system while our absence should result in energy shut-off. It might be somewhat childish to give an example – but my hybrid vehicle literally brings the revolutions of the engine to a crawling zero, and as soon as the foot is lifted off the breaks, the engine comes alive. It saves a little bit of gas in the larger scheme of things but this little bit is better than not saving any gasoline. Similarly every business must be given a schedule to get implemented a system of conservation with less warmth than laws require in the businesses today.

It is also the duty of the environmentalists to come up with better ideas to help the nuclear industry or any industry and conduct research so that a safe and truly inexpensive method can be used to produce vast amounts of electrical energy. They should help the United Nations draft an international law that no country will ever bomb a nuclear power plant as well as help create other safety measures that I cannot write here. It is the duty of the producers to operate these power plants in concert with the environmentalists so that a more cooperative atmosphere can emerge without jeopardizing the safety aspects of the operations. The city planners should also be invited to make sure that the public at large is not affected by the proximity of an unintended leak or something similar (sabotage).

5.6 Moral Responsibilities

The churches, the mosques, the temples all have a moral duty. I would love to see a sermon dedicated to the conservation of energy with specific quotes from the scriptures. If we elevate energy to the level of water conservation, and it is marginally less important, we should be able to quote from the teachings of all the religions. Please note that if we do not receive energy from the Sun direct or indirect, the oxygen based life as we know it will disappear. Muslims are required to perform ablution before praying and take a bath upon becoming unclean. Once a follower inquired from Prophet Mohammad (and I am paraphrasing); if there was such a thing as excess use and wasting water while performing ablution. The response was to the effect; *"Do not waste water, even if you perform your ablution on the banks of a richly-flowing river."* Clearly the message is to not waste anything that is a precious resource of the planet.

The moral responsibilities do not just belong in the religious sermons. They also belong in the homes, in the businesses, in the factories, and anywhere the energy resources are being consumed. It is not too much to ask the parents to emphasize conservation in the homes, teachers to teach in the classrooms, in the businesses to manage cash-flow and so on. This is one place where I wish to admonish my fellow citizens as well; that unless we stop and think about our insatiable appetite to buy bigger gas or electric guzzlers, our days of leading the world are soon to be over. I close by saying:

Energy is so precious it has been worshipped in the past. Let us make a real effort to produce clean energy and conserve what is being produced. Use the energy to explore the heavens and the Earth. Humans have to display wisdom and responsibility.

CHAPTER VI
Caring for the health of a Nation

6.1 Health Care System 101
A Health Care System begins to take care of an individual at conception and stays with that individual until his death. Now there may be societal functions before conception and after death as well but for the individual it is from womb to tomb. This system is always available with or without asking by the individual. So if an accident happens, the unconscious individual is rushed to the hospital without that person's consent. We have already discussed privacy issues. The system includes but is not limited to "providers" of a piece of or all of the components required in taking care of "humans". We will not address animals and other life forms in this chapter, which may be important in their own right. The providers are classified based upon what they provide. For example an insurance company provides insurance products to suit the needs of "subscribers" people who will be covered in case of an illness etc. to pay the charges billed by other providers. Similarly doctors, pharmacists, nurses, hospitals, Nursing homes, direct care staff, cleaning staff, and others are paid (sometimes they volunteer) to provide the services to the individual so that the process of rehabilitation from any illness continues until the quality of life of the person is fully restored or the individual dies. Ideally that is what a Healthcare System is supposed to do at a minimum. The higher quality health care systems also pay a great deal of attention towards prevention as in most cases it is far more inexpensive than cure.

In almost all the civilian cases the health care is provided at the State level. The doctors, for example, are required to have at a minimum a State License of the State they practice in and so on. In general if someone is brought to an emergency room for reasons that are classified as emergency room situation, the hospitals rarely refuse to treat the individual. So, for example, if a person is brought to the Bridgeport Hospital in Connecticut, and he is going through heart attack, he will be treated as fast as the hospital can – or at least I hope so. The hospital procedure will not begin by asking accounting questions about who is going to pay and who is covered by what insurance and so on. Similarly if a trauma victim is brought to any hospital, and if the hospital is equipped to provide the services, it will rarely refuse on financial grounds. But that is where the benevolence, thanks to the taxpayer and certain philanthropic organizations ends. So if you want to go for a physical examination to a hospital, you better have a way to either pay or lie like hell to make it an emergency situation, and there is a good chance your lies will come back to haunt you. Since a physical examination comes under prevention and quality of life care, you would think that any provider should jump at the chance every six months and the taxpayer should pay and since this will be for all, it will be a great equalizer. But that is not true in the United States. You must pay for your well baby and grown up care. This coverage of payment for services performed by the "providers" to the individual might be the first step towards a respectable level of health care in the Obama Administration.

In order to continuously provide better diagnostic equipment, drugs, and other product and services, research is in general conducted by scientists and engineers working for a provider, scientists and students working in a university setting, or just entrepreneurs. Medical Schools, Pharmacy schools, and a great many learning institutions contribute in the making of a doctor, a nurse, and hospital/nursing home administrators and so on. They are all part of a research arm of the Health Care System. The most important part of being able to cure something is to know that there is a problem, i.e. a great diagnostics system is essential. We must know how to measure blood pressure before we can keep high blood pressure under control using some medication. The next thing is to know whether a cure is possible, whether a cure exists, or is there an experimental treatment available courtesy some research organization. Part of the research team's job is to also find out all the risks associated with a specific treatment and so on. One of the crucial decisions a provider (in general a team of doctors, pharmacists, and nurses) has to make is whether or not the patient will survive the rigors of treatment itself. So the process of "research" is on-going to invent diagnostics equipment, blood tests, other chemical ingredients, and equipment and so on. Experiments to invent drugs, to conduct drug trials on humans and measure side effects are all part of this research. It further has to conjoin the actual research of correct prognosis and precise cure always keeping in mind that the process of rehabilitation does not stop till complete cure or death. If cancer is in remission, it is not enough to say well, now one can relax. Even after a full cure an ongoing examination is essential. This is all part of the research – the knowledge required to truly practice PCI and to keep increasing that base of knowledge upon which better and better palaces can be built. ***We end this section by recommending that all impediments in funding or otherwise be removed from STEM CELL research.***

6.2 The Next Twenty Years

All the "baby boomers" are headed for the emergency rooms, the hospitals, and the nursing homes in the next twenty years and we are not prepared for it. The government is "not responsible" and the families are unable to take care of their loved ones at home except for the extra rich, which I don't know how many will be left in the aftermath of all the Ponzi schemes that have been uncovered. I will carry a serious discussion of this topic and request president Obama for serious help, if America has to remain a leader in the space age medicines of the healthcare industry. Example: why is it that in old age there is degradation of muscle structure? And an Astronaut staying in space for extended periods has a similar problem. Is there a connection? Can we use the knowledge base to improve the quality of life of our elders on the surface of the Planet? Example: In human blood there are these "Heme Sites" that have the character of *absorbing oxygen* when it is plentiful, as in lungs, but reversing the process and releasing oxygen when it is in short supply, as in the remote parts of the body such as fingers and so on. Can we understand this better to retard the oxidation process and elongate life while improving quality as well?

There are a number of issues on the table for the Obama team when it comes to aging baby boomers. One that is near and dear to me is the total lack of care by the State and Federal agencies. For them, it is always about documentation and book-keeping and payments and imposing fines and never about patient care. The lack of care and funding of the poorest in the society is shameful when it comes to the older and mentally impaired population. We used to think that a very small number of people have any mental "illness" but now we know that almost four percent of the people are suffering from some form of mental infirmity. In terms of the numbers, it is about the same as the black population when Obama was a child. This is not good for the nation and the federal and state officials have no clue. Example: Once or twice a year some inspector(s) will arrive at a nursing home to look for flaws in the operation of the facility. They are not coming to help in any way. They are coming, looking, to see if an innuendo can be slapped, a deficiency is spotted, a "federal tag" can be generated or any blame can be laid so the direct care staff is intimidated. A few days later a bunch of papers shall arrive with allegations. If one wants to challenge the findings, the person has to go to the same people who were there to begin with. No independent body or "court" will hear the challenges. Their simple justification for everything is to repeat the mantra that we are doing this for the safety and security of the residents. The system is so wired that it is useless to try to fix the situation; either do what the agencies want, if you have a mission; If you don't have a mission, you are better off shutting down the facility and do something else in life than to be involved in the noble cause of helping the old and the infirm. In the meantime, the people who are in need of care can suffer while this bureaucratic mess is sorted out and the resources are applied for the solution of non-care type problems, including hiring of the lawyers, who themselves have long term relationships with these agencies and will not resolve anything quickly.

Taking care of the old and the weak is one of those areas that is in dire need of reform and does not require billions to fix; only careful evaluation and a few pennies will make the life of tens of millions so much better. In our humble opinion, aging and mentally infirm baby boomers should be given the highest priority and a non-profit and non-governmental agency such as Red-Cross appointed to resolve disputes in a helpful way. Some of these rules are so archaic that even if the services have been provided, and the money is available, internal agency rules are designed to make matters worse; and rather than making the rightful payments, are looking elsewhere to find faults. Of course if the ownership is engaged in fraud and criminal activity, the law enforcement should be informed. There is no need for incompetent agencies making life more difficult of the weakest in the society than it already is. Eliminate these agencies and give the money to Red-Cross to distribute directly to the residents or the legitimate folks taking care of them. If nothing else, enough money should be provided by the agencies to at least cover all the legitimate expenses. Remember that none of these people are insured by any private insurance company. We are making the following recommendations:

1. Appoint a federal commission to look at the fundamentals in as far as care of the baby boomers is concerned.
2. Arrive at recommendations to reform Federal agencies and their State agents (the State agents are usually State agencies) and cut their powers drastically. Appointments of "judges" from outside the system to resolve disputes must be one of those recommendations. Currently, one of the parties to the dispute is also the judge and the jury.
3. The Federal Government must significantly improve funding so that it is tied to the cost of care and increase in inflation at county level. We should stop telling people that there is an average cost of living increase across the country – that is a lie.
4. Remove the impediments in legitimate ownership changes and cost of replacement calculations and all the rules concerning "the lowest of the three, this or that". Stop all the impediments in bringing private funds to help the government for legitimate expenses and their return of investment.
5. Recognize truly that mental illness is legitimate and a comprehensive plethora of tests (more than a few simple psychological tests) be developed and research conducted to tie them to physical disabilities if any; be part of required tests so that funding can be increased for that individual . Currently, there is no tie between the Psychological doctor of the patient and their physician and this lack of understanding of the individual by the "team" providing care is very disturbing. This must be recognized and resolved.

6.3 Changing the Thought Process in Healthcare
In order to move to the future a change in the thought process is also required in the healthcare systems. The change has to be proposed and accepted by all sides. This includes consumers and providers. Each and every one in the system which is practically the population of the United States has to participate. Example: law-suit(s) against

doctors and hospitals cannot be ruled out but the frivolous lawsuits must not be allowed to destroy an entire field of medical science questioning the integrity and sincerity of the practitioners, hospitals and so on in that field and making insurance premiums go out of control. This state of affairs does not require additional funding in the system, it only requires political courage. Humanity is not at risk of becoming extinct and a level of sacrifice will only help the humanity on both sides of the issue. If there is criminal intent then all bets are off and the justice system must take over. But if an employee of a hospital is alleged to have spit in another employee's coke, it should not name the hospital as a defendant simply because the hospital has money but the employee who is not even guilty does not. The lawyer who is hell bent upon wanting a settlement from the insurance company is in fact suing the entire nation and the court is helpless but to accept the petition and the two sides fight it only because the hospital's employee insurance company will most likely settle instead of fighting all the way (as it is cheaper). The settlement usually results in a significant amount going in the attorney's pocket. Clearly it is about making money and nothing to do with concern for anyone, the justice, or any principle of justice. It is indeed an insurance system loophole, which must be closed.

Let us take another area which has to do with donation of human parts to improve some other patient's chances of living a bit longer. There is trade worldwide where poor of a country are lured into giving up their kidneys or whatever and die on the operating table only to be chopped up for the other parts as well. The governments of these countries have let the laws swing in the other direction to the point of oppression. Again if the United States and its allies absolutely forbid the trade of the human parts, it might hasten growing human parts in a laboratory. So this should be an area which might be of interest to Obama; increase significantly research funding not just on these types of issues but in all areas of human endeavor in medical sciences. Increase research funding is the cheapest way of solving a nation's problems regardless of the political climate.

Finally another area near and dear to my heart is the automation of the healthcare industry. The level of automation is archaic in this industry. What would I like? The easy things are already almost there, i.e. billing, accounts payable and receivables, diagnostics help, operating a magnetic resonance scanner, drugs on-line, statistical information and so. But even this is all way behind schedule. Take the example of Magnetic Resonance – it took medical profession for ever to recognize that physicist had discovered something many decades ago that humans can use for their cure. Take the example of nuclear technology; radiation treatments and their effects were know to physicists but the medical profession was just busy making money off the backs of patients. It is not just scientific research for the future that is slow to be understood by this industry. Example: Infection control inside the hospitals is a serious issue. The scientific methodology is well understood but the will to control this oddity is only half hearted. The hospitals of today are archaic and their very design is suspect in their ability to control infections. I am not in the business of finding faults – my only point is that the thought process has to change within Washington to take the nation in the field of medical science where it should be.

The one bright spot is research in new drugs. Here giant corporations are engaged in true scientific discovery for the benefit of both the humanity and their improved profits. However, the government's attitude, in particular FDA rules, tax benefits abroad, cheap labor and raw material are forcing some of them to look abroad to establish plants. This is unfortunate as it is the patients in the United States that are keeping them profitable. This is another area that needs to be looked at by the new administration think tank on the healthcare system if there is one.

Let me present a futuristic wish for the people in the United States. A person walks into a room that is really a "machine" installed into a pharmacist office. The machine examines him/her top to bottom and gives the person a complete diagnostic. It talks to the person and his/her doctor and dispenses medicine then and there, including a second opinion from a random doctor of the field, if need be. That is the change I am talking about; it is colossal but it can be done, not in a day but somewhere the start has to be taken. This might indeed be Obama, just lay the foundation of "out of the box" thinking in Washington; what better infra-structure than medical sciences.

6.4 Step by Step and a Steady Hand

Clearly the healthcare temple has many cogs every one more important than the other. Our suggestion will be to set up a commission which is not political in nature but consists of professionals which looks at the entire problem, then sorts out what can be fixed inexpensively, what requires medium level monetary commitment and what is truly a huge expense. Then within each category what can be fixed in the short term (less than four years), within eight years and what requires a longer term commitment (President Nixon knew that his cancer initiative will take longer than his term). Once it is presented to a larger group of people, it needs to be understood as to what can just be done by an executive order and what requires congressional passage.

One has to begin the mantra on changing the thought process, look for out of the box inexpensive solutions, on day one as the fixing of the healthcare system will ultimately require the nation to cough up a lot of taxpayer dollars. But this is where Mr. Obama comes in – he has to sell it to the nation and tell the people that it for the baby boomers, it is for their children, grand children and great grand ones too. The solutions are required to put the country on a path to victory over germs and viruses; and produce a truly healthy nation to cross the century leading the world and moving into cosmos.

CHAPTER VII
Political Reform

7.0 Self Reform

The most difficult thing in an individual's life is to "reform" himself (or herself). The more serious the problem, the more difficult it is to overcome. A bad drug addict needs external help - a locked up unit in a hospital and so on. Mr. Obama himself had to spend a moment or two thinking about quitting smoking or at least not to smoke inside the White House. Nation's leaders are addicted to certain political drugs. May be it is too harsh to say drugs, may be they are forced to take an elevator that only goes up and down and while inside an elevator their vision is impaired. To be able to lead is not easy, you have to have a vision set very high, your vocabulary to be elegant and the selection of the words as good as chosen by a great poet and most important you have love for the country second to none. Your political life revolves around a constant thought "what can I do to make the country better". All comparisons with Lincoln will fail if self reform is not a priority.

Similarly, on Congress, I would like to note that the politicians after having lived in Washington are addicted to certain ways. They must first reform themselves, if there is any chance of saving the nation from its bad habits. Will it be too harsh or childish that each congressional staff and members go through a "reform" training session on a monthly basis which inculcates in them what they may already have known? This training reinforces the fundamentals. It reiterates that even the minutest of the "moral" impropriety is unacceptable. If a self reform becomes a pre-requisite, it is a good start. Congress must not hear ethics allegations against members or the staff of the congress. It must appoint a strictly non-partisan body chosen by the Supreme Court or whoever. At this point no one is under suspicion in the new congress, why not this is the first thing that begins the change in the thought process in D.C. Let the gods say "be" and "it is".

7.1 Congressional Committees and Term Limits

Can the people of the United States appoint a committee to find out the structure of the congressional committees and what makes them so lucrative that any and all members want to be on the most "powerful" committee? Common sense dictates that the more senior a member is, the more secure his seat is, the more powerful position he gets on the committees; the least focused he is on the national problems. He is in a perpetual cycle to perpetuate him. Should there be a rule that says, the longer you are in the body the smaller will be your salary? And if you are there for sixty years you will get no pension. Can we simply ask the president to have as few secretaries as possible (or cabinet posts) and the number of these congressional committees be cut to that number or less. Can we simply ask the congress to at least have one committee dedicated to the Principle of Continuous Improvement and once in a blue moon state that what we thought was a good principle is not and begin to look at the consequences of that historic change?

Could we please be allowed to write about term limits for the Congress and the Senate? Congressional terms of two years are too small a time-frame. Here is a scientific reason; the subject matter on any good piece of legislation is too complex and requires reading. The member is too busy raising funds and the legislation does not get the attention it deserves. Members of congress are perpetually running for re-election and drawing fat salaries on top of that. Similarly why should the Senate term be for six years? Is it possible to look at the next two hundred years and see if the term limits are alright? Or is it too much to ask both the Congress and the Senate to reform them? Should we ask the nation to allow the creation of a fourth body that simply works for the nation and thinks about the reform of the democracy itself? This body elects one member from each States for life (like the Supreme Court members). I am unwilling to trust the current system that spends a life time re-electing itself. In my humble opinion, two four year terms for congress and two five years terms for senate are enough. You can come back after a four or a five year absence if you love this job so much.

Finally the budget of the congress has bloated itself too much, and has indigestions as a result. When was the last time that any cuts in congressional staff were announced and they suffered layoffs as a result of bad economy? If these congressional staffers and members are unable to manage the country's finances, and ask tough questions of the Executive branch, their salaries should be cut and their perks taken away. They are constantly having these hearings talking about huge CEO salaries; should they apply the principles on themselves.

7.2 Election Reform

This is an area touched a bit in the previous section in the context of term limits. The biggest weakness in the current system is that it is heavily tilted in favor of the incumbent. That starves the bodies of fresh blood, new and innovative ideas, creative thinking and a whole lot more. The approach in which the taxpayer funds the presidential or any other campaign is unacceptable to me. Similarly, a contribution coming from a political action committee, a directed effort of the members of a corporation, or any such entity that is anything but an individual should be disallowed. However, the individual member contribution may be raised a bit. This will keep everybody looking to find creative ways to *reach the maximum number of people* in their constituency rather than be subjected to lobbying entities and ensuing political corruption. Unless congress is willing to take these types of issues seriously, it is in danger of losing its prestige forever.

While there are legitimate exceptions, the nomination by the Governor of a State for a vacating Senate seat is invariably subject to political considerations and perhaps blackmail. If a seat becomes empty, it should only be filled by an election. The nomination, regardless of how qualified a person may be, does not belong in the legislative branch; as this further helps the entrenched and once nominated, the person becomes an incumbent and the action of the nomination is by definition against the spirit of democracy.

7.3

Executive Branch (Federal)

The most significant long term appointment(s) that a President makes are those of the judges of the Supreme Court. I am personally opposed to appointment of a judge that is based upon any political affiliation whatsoever and a litmus test of any kind. It has become a fashion to be asking about Roe V Wade and so on. It is quite possible that a nominee or a sitting judge can change their mind. If Roe V Wade is reversed, humanity will not become extinct that second, the fight will go on just as it is going on now. It is incumbent upon the President to bring those to the Court who have a history for thinking out of the box, a Pulitzer Prize winner, someone who has invented something or a famous scientist and so on.

Next, the current nominations of various secretaries are alright but the biggest issue facing the nation now is economics, and in my opinion, the most important qualification for any secretary (without exception) should be a deep knowledge of the economy. The defense secretary, can contribute a great deal if he has at least taken 101 economics. He/she controls one of the biggest budgets of the nation. I am at a loss that a nation that is facing a trillion dollars in budget deficit is keeping a large number of soldiers abroad. Bring them all home and get them working in education, in homeland security, in infra-structure development and the areas talked about elsewhere in the book. Set up alliances and let some of the other countries fill the shoes. If they need the United Sates, tell them to cough up money for providing security umbrella (does not have to be profit making mercenary type relationship) and soldier salaries etc... There is no shame in this type of arrangement. Clearly, when it comes to the defense of the United States, there is no cutting of any of the corners whatsoever.

An area that needs significant change is how economy is regulated. The current system clearly has failed and is archaic. It is based upon rules and laws that are "communist inverse". If I could write a formula, it will be Communist Economy times Communist Inverse Economy is equal to one. The United States needs laws that are not "induced" by Capitalism (i.e. Capitalism is neither for worship nor supreme), rather the laws are supreme and capitalism is checked at every level. The laws concerning futures trading and speculation in the commodities are not designed to propel a nation into cosmos nor of any real benefit to the longer term leadership development. The laws have to make some advancement to check greed and reduce oppression. The "cabinet" nominations (and their deputies and assistants) have to be of such caliber that they can inspire the best of the economists and physical scientists. Otherwise the thought process in Washington will never change. Mr. Obama alone cannot be the change agent; to his advisors, please make sure that he does not think that he is just about there with the Almighty and cause things to change by simply saying "be" and "it is".

7.4 The Supreme Court – Please Help

Let us examine this body as well. I personally think that this branch of our government is perhaps the noblest of the three. However, this does not mean that in this extreme environment when the entire nation is suffering from economic exhaustion, they can sit in isolation and not show some judicial activism in the economic arena in general and in the healthcare area in particular. The main reasons for me saying this branch is the noblest is them not being involved in a perpetual cycle of lies and elections. The nation has a tremendous respect for the highest seats of the judiciary and seldom cries fowl.

In the economic area, the Supreme Court may want to look at the whole notion of "future's trading", the underlying philosophies concerning "banking". What are the fundamental concerns in Capital Formation, and anything the economists would know a lot more than me. Similarly in the area of Health Care, the Supreme Court can play a very important role and help the new President and a nation looking to move forward. It will cut a whole lot of unwanted and unproductive thrashing around on issue after issue, if a single decision allows the nation to deduce so many productive rules. Would it not be a great decision, if the Supreme Court simply says that it is unconstitutional to not provide healthcare to anyone simply because to exercise any and all of the rights in the constitution, the person must be "healthy and of sound mind". Therefore the entire population must be covered by the "Federal Government" and its agents to ensure their health till death. God knows how many times frivolous lawsuits have been filed and the camaraderie of the lawyers on both sides has dragged these in the court system for years only to be shoved aside. For once perhaps the Court can simply say; healthcare will not be a political football.

7.5 Role of the Press

I must admit, that there are no new ideas when it comes to the role of the press in the United States. I know that the Principle of Continuous Improvement still holds and perhaps the changes are happening in front of us. The nightly news is no longer the way most people get their news and even the 24x7 news cycles have found plenty of competition on the internet. People question much more of the truth in a news story, the basis of their veracity and so on, than they used to, but the mundane news are still gathered by AP and so on. The news angling graduates, the slant masters, and the spin doctors abound. Interestingly, the press is all about selling a story to the people at large (they claim to be holier than thou but primarily it is to make money in the process).

In influencing war and peace, their role is primarily ineffective. The press and its components are still citizens of a country and the patriotic feelings do cloud their judgment. The press was mostly ineffective until the plans to spend a trillion dollars in the current wars had already seriously hurt the national economy. As an ordinary citizen (even though Muslim) I am unable to blame the press for the consequences of not aggressively going after the administration, when Paul Bremer made serious mistakes in Iraq. Notice that to me the two wars in Iraq and Afghanistan are predominantly domestic issues; so I have not even analyzed them in the chapter on foreign policy.

Also, the press is a self appointed organ of the people. No one has elected any of the anchorpersons. So their influence on the people is unjustified. They have also not been appointed by any elected officials (except for people who argue with them constantly such as the presidential press secretary and so on). Perhaps the technology will develop in such a way that each individual will have any and all the information available at the fingertips in a structured way - the information concerning the person, the family, the office, the city/town, the State, the country, the planet, and beyond. I believe that "very soon", all the pundits will be looking for more lucrative positions elsewhere in some other industry. When the history is finally written, in as far as press and its rise and fall, it will become clear that the press in its current form made many serious mistakes, and based upon the PCI, its influence declined and eventually disappeared. At the moment though, the Obama administration is well advised to keep cordial and friendly relations with the press, but remember that it is the people whose "well being" is the issue.

7.6 The Armed Forces

The political reform of the armed is in the hands of the civilians. My only request to these civilians is that they will make sure that the armed forces shall remain the best in the world, and they will not be sent in harm's way on a whim or fiction. That when they are sent to fight, the aim will be of a quick victory and exit while remaining magnanimous and merciful after the victory. My only hope and request from the military establishment is that every penny that they spend is well spent. We have to be ready to fight a star-wars scenario but the civilians will actually not deploy anything that is a provocation in the eyes of a world that is (not only) not ready but does not care about a fictional enemy. We should be friends with every nation on the planet and get ready to help in the exploration beyond. I have the utmost respect for the eighteen year olds who is ready to lay his/her life on the line for the nation.

There are a number of systems which are strictly offensive in nature. These systems should be looked at carefully and if the adversaries do not have a similar program to rethink the pace of development. The money thus saved should be spent on improving the basic military infra-structure such as hospitals and the care of the veterans, their mental health etc., coming home after years of missions. I believe that the civilian administration has a long way to go in establishing systems in which veterans are fully taken care of. I have personally dealt with veterans and their individual issues - where I have at times been very sad at the lack of care and monetary support at the individual level – there is always an excuse.

Let us prove to the world that there is strong motivation for self reform, and the nation has embarked on a journey in a well known direction for the next two hundred years. It is led and accompanied by those committed to a strong political reform at the congressional and executive levels. We are excited about the opportunity that nations of the world have given us and we will do whatever humanly possible to not disappoint them.

CHAPTER VIII
The Foreign Policy of the Unites States

8.1 The ABC of Foreign policy

For a president this is perhaps the most crucial area of long term policy making; beyond homeland security and God forbid a civil war if one is started or raging. I thank the Almighty that it is not the case. Let me first describe my view of the "theology" of foreign policy. For a country like the United States which asserts world leadership there are three important criteria for prioritization, or should I say triage, of tasks within the framework of "foreign policy".

a) The policies have to ultimately benefit the people and the country in a measureable way

b) The policies have to benefit the humanity at large, again with evidence based on data

c) The United States provides a mode of "prevention" rather than "cure" in making sure that peace is preserved; the country is a model to be adapted, is an accepted moral leader, and pushes the concept of "Principle of Continuous Improvement" for the humanity at large.

Even to achieve one of them the country has to be economically and militarily strong. If president Obama can accomplish all three, he will be a great leader. If he accomplishes two of the three he will be a good leader. If he just accomplishes the first of them, he is Ok. But if he reverses the course in any of the three, he will be a bad president. The situation he inherits is bad.

All indications are that a large majority of the people in the Islamic world (one-fifth of the population) dislike the United States. Another one-fifth (i.e. China) do not admire the policies of the United States; if anything reject them. Finally an additional one-fifth are ambivalent or simply do not regard America as a model country. A new paradigm is therefore sought from the Obama team. One that sets its goals to at least prioritize correctly the tasks at hand, is visionary, shows futuristic leadership, and not perennially reactive. Let me give you a common man's example: if I were to ask an ordinary guy in Timbuktu "Hey what do you think of America – give me two words"? And he says "cow boy" then something is wrong with our foreign policy. However, if he says "Neil Armstrong", then not only I like the answer, I tell president Obama to keep doing whatever it is you are doing. That is the essence of the foreign policy I am pushing for as a layman.

So before jumping into specific trouble spots around the world and pushing and shoving, a thoughtful understanding of the long term goals is required. Coming up with a vision spanning a century is required. This vision has to be as close to 20/20 as humanly possible. Re-arrange the chess board to not only think of the planet but beyond. Think of a world without war. Think of a permanent outer space human colony with perpetual replacements. We may not achieve any of the lofty goals but at least plan for them, look for alliances to architect, design, implement and quality control the infra-structure that takes humanity to the next plateau. The great leaders are liked by all. They all think that the leader is closest to them, rewards them for the good work, is charismatic, and while the leader is among them they all want to follow. Can America achieve all that – I think so.

So should the United States give any one country so much weight that a whole bunch of others think that the leader likes that one so much better than us; we are just orphans or worse yet, we have to form alliances against the United States and so on. Clearly China and India may be given more importance than the others but not because they are big and bullies in their neighborhoods but the United States require they share the same lofty goals and are willing to put their money where their mouths are. If that is not the case, if all they want is to slowly deprive us of our wealth, they have to go their way and we will go our way – but our way has to be measurably superior and they will eventually follow by example – we will welcome them at that moment.

8.2 Democracy is Not Utopia and it has a Long Way to Achieve Utopia

Our policy to export democracy by force is wrong. As mentioned elsewhere in this book, democracy is not an ideal form of government and unless we can continue to improve it, it too will follow the law of nature, the PCI, and wither away as before. Democracy is not Utopia but it has a pretty good chance of becoming so. We mentioned earlier several examples where democracy has failed us. Further, the moves to exclude religions and time tested morality in their entirety and proceed in an unknown direct ion, without a laboratory to practice the consequences over a longer term, are unacceptable. To continue unabated propaganda, and force democracy on people's throats as the salvation, while ignoring the time tested values in other cultures and countries will backfire. They will see drinking and prostitution rise, they will see state sponsored gambling become a nuisance, they will see significant increase in abortions and call it a murder and the list goes on. Therefore a gentle push towards democracy is more effective. It must be tailored and be country or culture specific. It must be an improvement over what they had in economy, in the lives of the ordinary people first before we can jump to lofty goals and an abstract freedom in which the only freedom someone has is to drink and make love and commit as much adultery and abortion as they want. It was not long ago that the Federal Government had no powers to take way federal income tax forcefully (except for the citizens of D.C.) and the lawmakers were appalled even at a 2% limit on federal income tax constitutionally. But a lack of constitutional amendment allows our federal government and the congress to keep playing with federal income tax merely to increase their salaries and some good works.

8.3 The Planetary Foreign Policy

In order to go beyond the intra-planetary country to country bickering, a foreign policy must be looked at against the paradigm of new hope and thought processes. What this means is very simple. If the countries can agree on some broad economic and trade pact, maritime laws, and so on, they can also agree on some principles which have all the hallmarks of "freedom". Once these are scheduled for implementation (say over hundred years) there should be no basis for the propaganda to overthrow this or that country's government; it should then be against international law in its final detail. If broad legal principles can be worked out the countries can tailor those principles based upon their environment and culture and move on to the real task of making real gains in people's lives. The point of this discussion is very simple. One cannot come up with phony excuses to go to war and occupying another country; then staying there forever by entering into an agreement with "their" phony leaders. *The acquisition of land and property by war must be abrogated explicitly by international law.*

8.4

Hot Spot One - The Israel Palestine Issue The land is ancient and the people are enterprising. Who else will be in a prison for better than sixty years and refuse to leave it or even pass-away? According to Mr. Carter, the former president of the United States, they have chosen to live in apartheid. The policy of the United States has been almost an unconditional support of the state of Israel. The State of Israel, by definition, can do nothing wrong, or so is the impression. We do not believe that this policy will change one iota with President Obama. I wish and pray that I am wrong even that much. Let me put it this way; suppose someone walked into your home and said "get out of this house it is really my home". You say "what the hell are you talking about. I have had this house in my family for four generations and I have been paying taxes". The guy calls in a bunch of thugs and shows a bunch of US made weapons and says "you leave

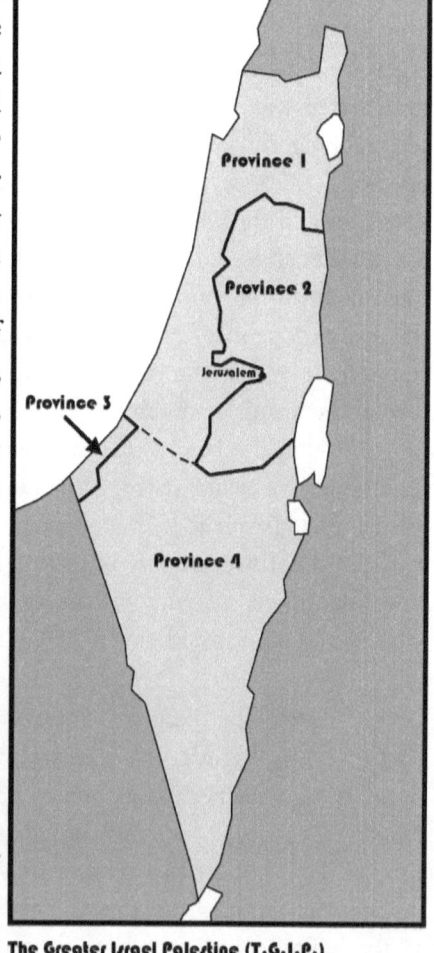

The Greater Israel Palestine (T.G.I.P.)

62

or I am blowing you and your family up in pieces". You leave the house and go to the police station and complain. The police officer says, "There is a new sheriff in town. He tells us that their ancestors lived here three thousand years ago. In fact they have been here since before the dinosaurs. So you have two choices - you can leave peacefully or will be made extinct like the dinosaurs – and we are about to do the same to everyone who has a house in this neighborhood. We are bringing a few more like them, spared by Hitler to take over your houses. You should know that there are people out there who are simply interested in making sure that the humanity keeps on fighting – World War II was not enough.

So with that the struggle begins and continues with attacks and counter attacks to this day. The money and more sophisticated weapons all continue to pour in from the United States. Propaganda calls anybody mildly questioning the oppression as a terrorist. I am waiting for someone to call Mr. Carter a terrorist. The vernacular changes but the violence continues. The two sides drift more and more apart. The Palestinians can never be treated with respect because one of them had a strange looking scarf covering his head. And even though, the biggest terrorist (as he was called) is dead the war goes on. It has been sixty years and I don't see it ending in the next thirty years (again I wish and pray that I am wrong). Now, if the United States continues to follow the current policy, it will never be able to establish a leadership role among the Muslim countries and the dictators and kings it relies on will all wither away and a new breed of youngsters that are Taliban like will take over the Muslim lands (and I wish and pray that I am wrong). Then I don't know what will happen – may be then the Muslims and the Christians will come together (I am praying that I will be right this time O God just answer my prayers once).

Having said all that, the children of the Jewish folks born in Israel and their children are also all sons and daughters of the soil. Any solution must treat them and their parents to be just as "Palestinian" or "Israeli" as the rest. I have seen humility and piety in some of them as well – yes O ye Muslims even in the Jews. I have seen this goodness among the Jews in the Bosnian conflict. They felt something inside them. They supported what was good and lend a hand in forbidding what was evil. Having seen this and much more, I have a simple suggestion presenting with utmost humility to both the Israelis and the Palestinians. It is to take the current

State of Israel and add to it Gaza and the West Bank, and call it the "The greater Israel and Palestine" TGIP for short. Then set up a UN supervised general election and elect a parliament of TGIP. The new parliament is charged under this UN mandate in coming up with a new democratic secular constitution based upon the simple principle of one person one vote over the age of eighteen. In the constitution, two additional "rights" should be added beyond the usual freedom of speech etc. First, the new constitution will allow any Jewish person to be treated as a citizen upon landing in TGIP from anywhere in the cosmos. Two, any "Real Palestinian "will have the same rights. I could further get carried away and propose four provinces two Jewish majority and two Palestinian majority and all this talk of border demarcation will go away. I see that if peace comes, then the new State could attract new immigrants and its population swell to twenty million – an exemplary state for the world. I know that neither Israel nor Palestinians will accept this concept, but I had to sincerely present the idea – may be they have better ideas? This proposed two state solution will not work ever. Those who think it will work are living in fool's paradise. One crisis after another shall keep coming.

If it is not possible to have a multi-religious State – and it had to be the Jews in control of the one side of the "mountain" and jointly the Muslims and Christian Palestinians of the other, then something is wrong with humanity itself. You see there is something to be said about the thoughtful Christians – may be they can come together in America with Muslims – that will also produce peace in the holy land and convince the eldest brother to relent. But then what will happen to the die-hard believers of the coming of Jesus (in their lifetime!) who are hell bent on killing every Jew in sight who will not convert; sounds like the one sided mindset of the government of the United States in its support of the state of Israel – tell them that my suggestion about TGIP will convince Jesus to postpone his visit for another two thousand years – peace would have broken out. My apologies to all the *humans* for this and the previous paragraphs, if I have offended them.

8.5 Hot Spot Two - The Issue of Kashmir

Let us now move to another hot spot called Kashmir that has remained a dispute between India and Pakistan for just as long. I have never criticized India and always praised the country. I have constructively criticized the country called Pakistan out of love and my first book in "Urdu" is a proof of that. In fact that is where the idea of PCI was first introduced without using the vernacular. There the concept of measuring time independent of the Sun and the Moon (and using internal unperturbed cycle of the human clock) was first introduced. Since I have significantly more knowledge of the area, I shall cover the dispute and present the solutions in far more detail than in the case of Palestine. The two should not be compared in my humble opinion as we shall see. The only similarity is that they are both a symbol of human weakness in the twenty-first century.

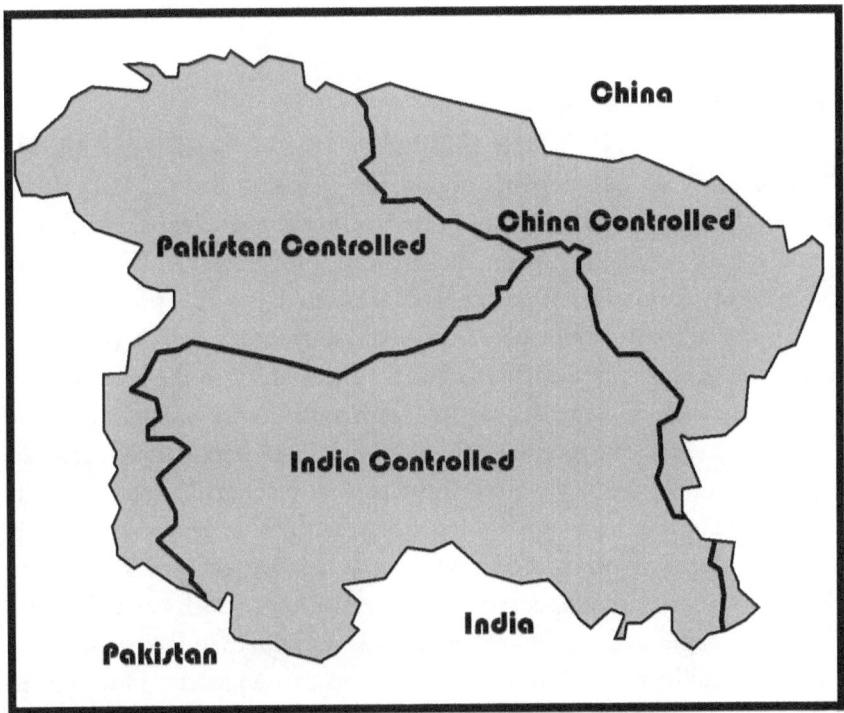

Kashmir Region

The first thing to realize in the Kashmir dispute is that India and Pakistan both recognize each other as (albeit belatedly) a sovereign country – one does not occupy the other. They both have embassies in the other country and both have a significant direct trade. There is road, railroad, and direct air service, and at any point a number of citizens are in the other country without being harassed. Compared to India, Pakistan is small (India is four times larger in area and eight times larger in population). However, Pakistan is still one of the largest countries in the world with a population of almost 172 million (compared to India's 1.15 Billion), the sixth largest in the world after China, India, United States, Indonesia, and Brazil. Both countries have nuclear arsenal and are not going to fight a real war (God willing?) regardless of what anyone says about them. However, the dispute of Kashmir is real and is the cause of certain deep economic concerns for both countries.

One of these concerns is the equitable distribution of waters of the five rivers that flow into the heartland of Pakistan. Let us examine the issue in some detail.

8.5.1 Introduction

In May 1974 India exploded a small nuclear device partly in response to geopolitical needs and a desire to show the world that it has come of age. It also wanted to let Pakistan know that the issue of Kashmir is practically dead (please refer to UN Security Council Resolution 47 - Documents No. S/726 dated 21 April 1948 etc.) And that Pakistan should never think of confrontation with India ever again. The timing was particularly bad for Pakistan since the memories of the 1971 debacle of East Pakistan was fresh in the minds of Pakistanis. The leadership in Pakistan was now convinced that its independence is at stake, and the country will be exposed to the nuclear blackmail which, from its point of view was no longer an issue between the "super" powers. Pakistan began to work on its own program at a heightened pace. The United States was particularly opposed to the acquisition of such capability and Henry Kissinger had tried to persuade and warn the then Pakistani Prime Minister, Zulfiqar Ali Bhutto, of unforeseen consequences. However, in December 1979, Afghanistan was invaded by the Soviet Union, changing the political landscape altogether. The United States actually began to look the other way as Pakistan continued to acquire Uranium enrichment capability during the unfortunate war in Afghanistan as a result of the Soviet invasion. The Reagan Administration had decided to ignore the nuclear issue and President Reagan had himself made the point that Pakistan was surrounded by Atomic Powers and rouge states. Simultaneously, India was proceeding on its slow but steady program of nuclearization and wanted to test the Hydrogen Bomb.

During the first Bush Administration it was apparent that Pakistan had the necessary materiel to explode the bombs and President Bush was convinced that "cold tests" have been conducted in early eighties. The US policy of non-proliferation including "Pressler amendment" (Nuclear Proliferation Prevention Act of 1994, Sec.902. Nuclear Non-Proliferation Conditions on Assistance for Pakistan, Section 620E of the Foreign Assistance Act of 1961) and congressional pressure stopped the sale of crucial defense equipment needs of Pakistan. This however, had exactly the opposite effect, pushing Pakistan further towards reliance on the atomic arsenal. Despite all of these developments Pakistan did not want to explode the bomb to avoid world's antagonistic reaction and the economic consequences.

When India exploded its Hydrogen Bomb along with four smaller atomic devices in May, 1998, Pakistanis had no choice but to quickly respond with their own explosions of (six) smaller Atomic Bombs "to even the account" (i.e. if you count the 1974 explosion by India). The Pakistani explosions had become essential strictly from a psychological perspective for the nation, since India and the world already knew the capability.

These explosions pushed the world closer to the dooms day (nine minutes to midnight as fixed by the journal "Bulletin of the Atomic Scientists", University of Chicago, June 1998) on the clock which has been main-tained since 1947. This came about due mainly to the disputed territory of Kashmir between India and Pakistan. Kashmir has thus emerged as a dispute not only to be resolved in the context of India and Pakistan but also essential to the peace and prosperity of the world at large.

8.5.2 Nuclear World's view

There are four parties to the conflict as a result of both India and Pakistan becoming nuclear powers. The parties being the people of Kashmir, India, Pakistan, and the world commu-nity at large, as they will all be engulfed quickly in any nuclear confrontation. Further analysis requires that we examine the political stance of certain countries. We will first examine the accepted five declared nuclear powers, at least before Indian and Pakistani explosions. The United States has the honor of being the first nuclear and perhaps still the sole "superpower", at least for a little while, but has never quite figured out on how to deal with India. It was clearly in favor of the United Nations resolutions in

1948 calling for a vote, and for the people of Kashmir to determine their fate on whether or not they want to live with India. While it believed in a certain balance of power between India and Pakistan, it could never allow Pakistan to become strong enough as it also thought of India as a counter to China. This was never more apparent than during the brief skirmish between China and India in 1962. The US public posture continues to be on the non-proliferation of atomic weapons. It is unclear whether it also continues to pay a lip service to the right of self-determination of the people of Kashmir. At the same time, though, it supports the Indian postulate that all matters are local and only dire circumstances such as one country taking over the other will trigger any real response. So it supports the Indian position of dialogue between India and Pakistan to resolve Kashmir and any other matter. India likes it this way and thinks that the people of Kashmir will forget and forgive India for all the atrocities committed by half a million troops and Pakistan will eventually give up as well. This is wishful thinking as history has proven time and again, be it anywhere in the world.

The former Soviet Union, like India, never quite understood the political division of India in 1947. Here, a shift is possible due mainly to the breakup of the Soviet Union. The former soviet states like Kazakhstan, Turkmenistan, Tajikistan, and others no longer give unqualified support to the Indian position. Russia, however, continues to give India the unqualified support at least publicly. It also continues to provide the most sensitive ballistic missile technology to India. It is this technological partnership between India and Russia that Pakistan and other countries such as the United States are worried about. India has other ambitions, falling in areas where space exploration blurs with military stuff such as espionage capabilities in any satellite technology. The Pakistanis, in the context of the former Soviet Union, also did not vigorously contest the salesmanship of India on the issue of Kashmir. The little thaw between Pakistan and the Soviet Union came in 1965 after President Ayub accepted the Soviet mediation in Tashkent after the seventeen days war between India and Pakistan. Pakistan never exploited this opportunity. The folks in Pakistan have not genuinely used the Central Asian states to their advantage to not only improve relations with the Russians, but also to let India understand that Pakistan has a choice and it can align its destiny with the states west of it not just India.

Next, China is playing an increasing role in the security arrangement of the Asian Continent Some think tanks in the West now regard China to be the superpower of the twenty-first Century. The historic relationship, which began with the recognition of the Chinese government by Pakistan in 1949, has continued to flourish and survived several tests of real and cold war's. The Chinese have also faithfully stayed with the Pakistani position on Kashmir from the beginning. The fact is that the Chinese for reasons that are both historical and geopolitical regard Pakistan's view on Kashmir to be closer to the "just" position and in their own national interest. The 1962 war between India and China further cemented the Pakistani position on Kashmir in the minds of the Chinese. As we have indicated above, a new equation is in the process of being formulated. The former soviet republics bordering Afghanistan and China are far more interested in seeing the war in Afghanistan end. They are also beginning to look to the east and realize that the China/Pakistan relationship can be very beneficial to the development of the region, and want to see the Kashmir issue resolved.

The United Kingdom has and continues to suffer from the guilt of the division of India as well as not resolving Kashmir and running away from the scene. It remains essentially uninvolved and has shied away from any real mediation effort either on her own or in conjunction with the United States. Due mainly to political clout India continues to enjoy a more favorable stance with the United Kingdom. The other reason is of course economic and India is still looked as having a much larger potential than Pakistan even though none of the companies in the United Kingdom have made any real money. It is indeed sad since United Kingdom still has immense influence in the context of the Commonwealth. For sure, the politicians know well that a vote for the self-determination in Kashmir will not go in favor of the Indian position. Perhaps the position of the United Kingdom can be best explained by simply saying that India does not consider the United Kingdom a first rate power anymore, and is unlikely to listen to it which I believe is not so.

The fifth atomic power, France, never quite got involved in this affair and simply remains happy by exporting Mirage fighter technology to both countries.

Until now, NATO as a North Atlantic Treaty Organization had little or no real interest in what goes on in the Indian Ocean region. This was a treaty framed as a bulwark against the Warsaw pact countries and mainly for the defense of Western Europe. There are other alliances but not quite as powerful as NATO. The action it has taken against Serbia without the express approval of United Nations speaks for itself. This is important to note that the action against Serbia, and now in Afghanistan, is not because Serbia or Afghanistan committed an aggression against any of the NATO member countries. It is based upon non-tolerance of gross violations of human rights, which is what goes on in the valley of Kashmir. But even more important to note, is that NATO also worries about defending itself against those states, which have the potential of targeting member countries with nuclear missiles. It is therefore, now interested in what goes on in the Indian Ocean region. In particular, NATO countries are alarmed that both India and Pakistan are engaged in a tit for tat policy of increasing ballistic missile ranges, which will ultimately be able to target any point on the globe.

The United States Congress is again funding the old "Star Wars" project pushed by President Ronald Reagan during Cold War. This means that there is sufficient concern not only among the non-governmental organizations and think tanks but also in the US Congress that the missile race is on, and eventually this technology will find its way to any country bent on acquiring it. NATO will play a crucial role in the eventual deployment of any such technology. Unfortunately, the more advanced nations of the East will try to develop an anti-Star-War technology and the race will continue in the outer space making space exploration a dangerous game. It is for these reasons and others that the issue of Kashmir has acquired a much more center stage position than it was before and Mr. Obama has mentioned Kashmir in his race to the White House – good thought for the peace of the world.

8.5.3 The Islamic Factor

Those countries where there is a majority Muslim population, the people (not necessarily the governments) are naturally inclined to believe that India is suppressing the Muslims similar to what Slobodan Milosevic was doing at a much larger scale in the former republic of Yugoslavia. The integrity of India, according to the Indian leaders must be maintained at all costs. The argument being that India is ethnically and linguistically so diverse that any crack in the alliance will result in a much larger bloodshed than just in Kashmir. Thus the political and sometimes violent struggle of the people of Kashmir continues facing India and Pakistan, with possible nuclear catastrophe for the world at large.

Whether we like it or not, whether it should be this way or not, the fact is that the explosions of the atomic bombs by Pakistan has had a tremendous psychological impact on the Muslim population throughout the world. When an Egyptian cleric leading the Friday prayers, in the United States, tells the parishioners coming from every part of the world, to be proud and celebrate this day, which elevates the "nation", tells the story. Ordinary Muslims and many intellectuals have felt that there was a conspiracy against them in that Israel and India could possess any arsenal including the atomic bomb, and the only option available to the Muslims was to live as second class citizens in world politics. In their simplistic notion, the destruction of the Iraqi nuclear installation [under construction] by Israel was a clear proof. They were unwilling to buy the argument that the democracies of the world must ensure that countries ruled by dictatorships must be off limits to these instruments of mass destruction. In any case, the point here is that over time, some of these Muslim countries may look to Pakistan for a security umbrella. What impact it will have on India is unclear. But what is clear, is that, India cannot improve its position vis-à-vis Pakistan in the battle of capturing the Muslim public opinion on the issue of Kashmir.

It should also be kept in mind that it is not just the majority Muslim countries where India faces an uphill battle for the minds of the people. But, in many western nations, Islam has propagated peacefully negating many myths and already become the largest religion after Christianity. Examples include England, France, as well as the first nuclear power, the United States, in spite of the violent terroristic attacks of 911. It is ironic that the Islamic thought and philosophy, despite relentless propaganda has had the opposite affect and Islam has become more popular in the west for a variety of reasons. For example, in the United States, the blacks have felt that their origins are Islamic and the "martyrdom" of people like Malcolm-X has produced sympathy for Islam. The immigrants from Pakistan to the

United States have been at the forefront of such an understanding of Islam. It is this factor as well that favors Pakistan and the people of Kashmir.

Finally, in an article published in the "Defense Viewpoint" (Volume 10, Number 10), William J. Perry, former US Secretary of Defense, writes "Today, each of them has the capability to build nuclear weapons. Because of this nuclear capability, a fourth India–Pakistan war would be not just a tragedy - it could be a catastrophe." He further quotes John Kenneth Galbraith who was serving as the US ambassador to India in 1962 as having told President John F. Kennedy that "Politics is not the art of the possible. [Rather, it] consists in choosing between the disastrous and unpalatable". The stance of India and Pakistan on Kashmir is unpalatable (it is also unpalatable on the issue of nuclear proliferation, but that is a different issue). But, for the world to use it as a reason to disengage from the Kashmir issue will indeed be disastrous from the point of view of this author as well.

In fact it can be argued that, at stake is the future course of economic development of the world, space exploration, and beyond, and not just the strategic relationships of today. Even if sufficient understanding exists between India and Pakistan, the thorn must be removed and the infection cured. Otherwise, the cancer will eventually engulf the world at large. The entire planet must be regarded as one body when the cancer is nuclear.

8.5.4 THE NON-NUCLEAR OPTIONS

As we have said before, the nuclear option is not an option; it is merely a deterrent. It is indeed mutually self assured destruction doctrine being played all over again between the cold war rivals. While some analysts may go into an esoteric debate on whether or not a nuclear war is winnable by either side and try to calculate the cost of such stupidity down to the ninth decimal place. It is not in the interest of a single soul capable of understanding the disaster. We are thus forced to take a look at the non-suicidal solutions. Wars, including armed revolutions, have solved some problems in the past including the overthrow of tyrannical governments. One such example on which most of us will agree is that of the defeat of Hitler's Nazi Germany. But it would have been a disaster of grand proportions if Hitler had the atomic bomb long before the allies did. It would have taken centuries to reverse the direction of the dark side of the human progress. One must look to the future, far in the future, to figure out what is really important for the human race. The NATO operation in Kosovo is a good example where ethnicity cannot be allowed to be the basis of rule of law. And the United States and the allies have gone to war over that issue asserting the principle. War cannot however be the vehicle in every case. One must examine the overall cost in terms of the human principles as well misery.

In Kashmir, the only principle involved is the forceful annexation of a territory regardless of the wishes of the people of that State. India has annexed several states into its territory forcefully. The examples include the States of Junagarh, the Sate of Hyderabad, and lastly the State of Sikkim. None of these states border Pakistan. But the main reason why India has gotten away with "police actions" is because the people of these states could identify themselves with the rest of India and the predominant culture, religion, and ethnicity could not be used as the basis of discrimination. It is sometimes argued that if the Congress Party led by Pundit Nehru had agreed to properly safeguarding the rights of the Muslims in the undivided India, then the partition of India itself could have been avoided. The Muslim minority in India has suffered heavily at the hands of the majority since its independence. The people of Kashmir (not all) have seen it and rejected India's claim over the State, regardless of what happened in 1947. The proof of this thesis lies in the very fact that India is afraid to let the United Nations take control over the territory and conduct fair and impartial polls. Pakistan has never objected to the salient features of such a proposal. Below we will examine and analyze the only five possible scenarios, which can be the basis for a lasting peace in the region. We will also examine why and which parties are opposed to any of these solutions. Since the damage has already been done, it will take careful preparation and selling of any of these proposals to the people of Kashmir as well those of India and Pakistan. Any effort not sincere and carefully planned will fail miserably and create its own set of problems and have the potential of getting out of hand. As we shall see below different options have their own unique set of issues and carry with them plenty of opportunity for mischief both within and outside.

a) CURRENT LINE OF CONTROL SOLUTION The most talked about option on the problem of Kashmir is to declare the current line of control as the international border between India and Pakistan. There have been rumors to the effect that once or twice the two countries have seriously talked about this option during the administrations of Rajiv Gandhi and President Mohammed Zia-ul-Haq, as claimed by Gandhi but not before Zia-ul-Haq died in a plane crash. Regardless, no leader, either in India or Pakistan will reveal the precise plan, as changes might be desirable by both sides to make minor adjustments from a population as well as defense perspectives. There are serious reservations about this proposal in both countries. The most important objection is really from the people of Kashmir who see their State being divided without their consent. In the current political atmosphere the people of Pakistan as well as of India are also opposed to the concept. There are two main reasons for this. In India, for over sixty years the people have been fed the party line, that Kashmir really belongs to India, and not just the part that it occupies but also the part that is under the de-facto control of Pakistan. And so if one speaks in the Indian heartland, he thinks that people of Kashmir really want to live in India and that Pakistan has occupied this piece of land illegally. The Indian press and successive administrations have never told them that if there was an independent election held under the UN supervision, that in all likelihood the people of Kashmir would reject the Indian occupation.

There are roughly half a million Indian troops engaged in keeping their side of the territory under control. The actual army which faces the Pakistan army on the other side of Line of Control is perhaps not even half that. There is no real government in Kashmir except what is imposed by India from time to time and the elections are a farce. Thus the biggest hurdle faced both by India and Pakistan is to convince the people of Kashmir that this option is the right long term option. And even if the two countries reach an agreement, the trouble will continue with in the Indian occupied Kashmir. It will also be a hard sell in both the countries and the two parliaments may never ratify the agreements, toppling the governments. This would require longer term and proper democratic processes to bring the people of both countries along and admitting sixty years of propaganda and counter measures on both sides. What is also difficult is the fact that despite India's bravado, both countries are poor and any effort to rebuild the shattered economy of the region, in particular of Kashmir, will require massive capital influx under any solution.

b) SOLUTION BASED UPON THE WISHES OF THE PEOPLE OF KASHMIR The second possibility for a solution in the State of Jammu and Kashmir is to accept the wishes of the people of the state. This can be accomplished in several ways. The most acceptable to India would probably be on the basis of a non-UN sponsored bilateral agreement between India and Pakistan. The most difficult part will be to determine the boundary in which the elections will be held under the watchful eye of a third party such as the United Nations. Note that the agreement can be bilateral but certain parts of the execution of agreements may still require a third party to ensure objectivity and honesty. The essential elements of such an agreement would require the inclusion of the "elected representatives" of the people of Kashmir. In broad terms there will be three phases of such an agreement. First, an agreement between India and Pakistan to accept the principle of "free elections" in the State and determine the boundary on both sides of the Line of Control for such an execution will go a long way. Second, with the help of a third party preferably the United Nations conduct free elections in a multi-party environment using a census mechanism approved by the Election Authority (i.e. the United Nations), India, and Pakistan. Third, on the basis of the results, boundaries can be established once and for all between India and Pakistan. There might be a cooling off period before phase one, a kind of phase zero. In our judgment this cooling off period has to be part of a grand scheme of things. Measurable goals will have to be set up and a fixed timeframe imposed for the specifics of the peace plan to have completed in this timeframe. A mere cooling off period which does not deal with the Kashmir issue is bound to fail. Some Western Governmental officials and "think tanks" suggest a cooling off period, in which the issue of Kashmir simmers, is not being proposed by us, since it merely prolongs the inevitable. The two countries must face this problem as part of the overall normalization. Next, the ballot should be totally objective. The three questions should be total independence, statehood within India, or a Province of Pakistan. In case there is no majority on the first ballot, a second vote can determine the outcome with a majority vote. While this option might be the most undesirable for both India and Pakistan, it is one that would be the fairest to the people of Kashmir. Both India and Pakistan need not fear the outcome.

It should be noted explicitly that only a fair and equitable solution will usher an era of goodwill and prosperity for the people of the sub-continent. The last sixty years of distrust which began even before gaining independence in 1947 cannot be wiped out if a significant population of both countries feels that the agreement is no good. And Kashmir is the one problem, which will not go away simply by wishing it. It has not happened in sixty years, and it is very unlikely to happen now. However, if the people of both countries are convinced that the solution reached is the best possible, then it is very likely that over time they will forget the bad feeling of the last sixty years, not in a day of course. An agreement along these lines will also bring very good economic news for both countries. While India continues to insist that its nuclear program does not revolve around a security threat from Pakistan only. It looks north to China as not only a nuclear power but conceivably also a super power in the twenty-first century. It feels with some justification that India is a great nation in its own right, and it cannot be treated as a backward nation in the same time frame. However, we feel that the psychological greatness cannot be justified without India becoming a great economic power as well. This cannot be achieved without a solution to the border problems that India has with China and Pakistan. And, of course, the biggest of these problems, and one which takes away most precious resources of India is the Kashmir problem, where an estimated half a million troops are tied down with the people of Kashmir. This is not just an armed conflict, but an entire population is sick of Indian behavior and human rights violations.

It can also be safely argued that Japan has more clout than India in global terms. It is certainly a great economic power (per capita and GDP). Japan's greatness under the security umbrella of the United States and slow movement to account for its own defense will be a check on the Chinese power at least in the next century. The theory that India can somehow do it alone just does not make sense. In the known history also, the Chinese have never marched on to the Indian Territory. Tibet is more of a religious freedom issue and deals with the intricacies of separation of Church and State, valid for all of China, than any "border dispute" with India. The problems of border dispute with China are relatively easy since almost no populations are involved. It is therefore, our opinion that economic greatness of India cannot be achieved and India cannot become a true super power without being friendly with both Pakistan and China. The journey begins by solving the Kashmir problem.

c) THE 1948 UNITED NATIONS RESOLUTIONS

The main difference between this and the previous section is the timing of the United Nations involvement. It is India's insistence that all matters including the key issue of Kashmir be settled bilaterally. Pakistan has been talking about the United Nations resolutions on Kashmir simply because it wants to show that it is on a higher moral ground. The fact also is that Pakistan agreed to a bilateral possibility during the so-called "Simla agreement". This agreement was reached at an hour when Pakistan had been defeated in a civil war with India's direct help in which East Pakistan became Bangladesh. The chances of a United Nations brokered deal are almost zero. However, as in previous section, if India and Pakistan can reach a bilateral agreement on the crucial issue of getting a free and impartial arrangement of a referendum, the United Nations resolutions can then serve as the basis for a vote. In terms of this particular option (UN resolutions) as a basis for conflict resolution, the author does not insist on ruling out bilateral agreements as a new leaf to resolve the matter. However, as indicated earlier, mechanism must be set up to conduct and monitor the outcome of the elections under those bilateral terms. We will end this section with news brief from Reuters, in which it is plenty clear that the people of Kashmir must be included in any settlement.

SRINAGAR, June 10, 1999: Kashmir's leading separatist alliance said today that it rejected the line dividing the region between India and Pakistan. "The state's Line of Control, which divides Kashmir, is like a blood line and we reject it," A senior leader of the All Parties Hurriyat Conference told a news conference. Abdul Ghani Lone also dismissed talks set for Saturday June 12th, 1999 between India and Pakistan and said they would have no meaning without the Hurriyat's participation. The group includes nearly two dozen political, religious and separatist groups in the Indian held Kashmir. "This is our problem, we have offered sacrifice of thousands of people and the dispute is on our land.... Whenever there is dialogue on Kashmir it should be trilateral," Lone said. "Our boys have crossed this line since 1990 because they don't respect the sanctity of the line and consider the whole part (Indian and Pakistani controlled Kashmir) their land. We appeal to people of Kashmir not to respect Line of Control but reject it," he added. Police and hospitals say more than 25,000 people including Kashmiri mujahedeen and Indian security forces have been killed and thousands wounded in Jammu and Kashmir since 1990. (Reuters)

d) THE SEPERATION OF JAMMU FROM THE VALLEY

There have been newspaper reports that some "think tanks" and United States government officials believe that in the State of Jammu and Kashmir, there is majority within a larger majority. In Jammu, which is a small part of the State, a slight majority of Hindus may want to stay with India. Perhaps, the thesis can be explained using the Irish example. There is a Protestant majority within Northern Ireland, but in the context of larger Ireland, this protestant majority is a small minority. The situation would be hopeless if United Kingdom were to insist on ruling the entire island of Ireland. Thus the argument put forward by some in the United States that perhaps the State of Jammu and Kashmir can be carved out between India and Pakistan in such a manner that the Valley of Kashmir becomes part of Pakistan, while the area around Jammu can continue to be part of India. While on paper, it appears to go along with the wishes of the people of Jammu and Kashmir there is no certainty. If indeed the thesis is correct, it can easily be tested in a vote. India has once rejected this as a basis for solution. Recently some life has been put into it. The issue again will be one of India even acknowledging that there is more to it than Pakistan simply sending mercenaries to fight and create an artificial armed struggle.

There are also suggestions that a Camp David style marathon parley should be held and the issue resolved once and for all with the United States supplying the "environment" as the two sides work out their differences. Neither India's nor that of Pakistan's entrenched interests will allow that to happen. But the larger issue remains the basis upon which a parley would occur. If the basis is to simply declare the current Line of Control as the international border, then they need not come to Camp David. The people of Kashmir will simply reject this solution and the struggle will continue. On the other hand, if the basis is the United Nations resolutions, both the people of Kashmir and Pakistan will welcome that. This will, however, be vetoed by India; again no need to come to Camp David. The only possibility is to start the negotiations without a basis and in the presence of the United States officials who would presumably be more objective; as no one in the US wants to see the two sides destroy world peace based upon nuclear Armageddon. It is clear also that India will never agree to any of these possibilities. In effect, the Indians want to use their nuclear power status to keep status quo. If indeed this is correct, then Pakistan as well as the people of Kashmir will continue their course. In fact, even if Pakistan were to agree to a Line of Control based solution, the people of Kashmir will reject it. It will merely prolong the agony of the people struggling in Kashmir, and in the next upheaval, things will be back to square one.

e) CONCLUSIONS

We will summarize our thought process by noting that given a very real nuclear threat, it is incumbent upon India and Pakistan to bring themselves together to resolve the long and complex issue of Kashmir. It might seem farfetched but even if India ends up relinquishing control over Kashmir either as an independent entity or some accommodation with Pakistan with the help of the legitimate representation of Kashmiris, India still ends up the winner in the longer-term. As we have indicated earlier, the Earth is poised for a larger world peace, as we prepare to take the human legacy in the Space and beyond. As part of this conclusion, we are also proposing a scenario, which is very likely to happen if India and Pakistan fail to bring themselves and the Kashmiris together. The example of cold war and communism is in front of us. It took over seventy years for communism's bulwark to finally disintegrate quickly. The internal pressure along with continuous external poking burst the bubble.

8.5.5 A LONGER TERM VIEW

The people of this planet are preparing to move to outer space for a number of reasons, and it is not for us to fully document them here. But as we all know, the new Space Station is an example of how America and Russia (the old rivals) are cooperating with several other countries to build this "first joint colony". Ultimately, there will be just a few major blocks in the world (the North American, the European, and at least one Asian) that will be in the forefront of this race, and we might add, peacefully. In order for India to join this race, it has to choose one of these blocks. Therefore she needs to join hands with all the countries of the region including China and Pakistan to move ahead. The first step towards such a goal is to strengthen the economic alliance of all the "nations" of the sub-continent itself. Even if Kashmir were to become independent, it has to exist within that alliance. India being the largest entity within this economic alliance would logically assume the necessary leadership, if it chooses to do so. Thus in the end, economic interests will overcome any short-term political as well as defense based alliances, as the future of the sub-continent lies together. There is a small start in the form of SARC (South Asian Regional Council) designed to promote economic cohesion of the region. Pakistan despite unfavorable conditions due mainly to the high Indian import tariff rates has joined the Council to show that it is interested. But any real progress cannot be made until the killings stop and the politically charged issue of Kashmir is resolved. India knows this well, but believes that using such vehicles as the World Trade Organization, it can move ahead and forge the economic alliances by hook or by crook.

Let us also assume that India does not want to exercise the option of solving the Kashmir problem. In that case Pakistan, unlike India, still has an option and its future can still be very bright. It will just take slightly longer, and may in fact be a better option. It has the option of joining hands with the countries to its West and the North namely China, Iran, the former Soviet Republics, Afghanistan, and others. In approximately one hundred years, Pakistan can integrate its economy with this larger alliance, countries with rich natural resources. It can provide the necessary security umbrella as well as human talent to create a block sufficient in size both in terms of area, population, and the resources. In this manner it can successfully compete in any space race vis-à-vis any other world block. And, it can keep the Kashmir issue alive. There is clearly no loss of cultural identity for Pakistan in joining hands with the people of these countries. Except for China, the other countries mentioned have had close linguistic and cultural ties for hundreds of years with what is now Pakistan. As far as China is concerned, as we have indicated earlier, Pakistan was one of the first countries to recognize China in 1949. The political friendship has stood the test of time for sixty years now. In fact, Pakistan played a key role in bringing China and the United States together, and the historic visit of Henry Kissinger occurred from Islamabad to Beijing. Clearly, the Chinese also value Pakistan's friendship. They have even shared in defense related technology. It will only be natural, if the alliance of Pakistan, China, and the West Asian States began to develop their own airplanes, shuttles, and commercial rockets with joint marketing agreements to bolster their chances of competing in the space age with the North American and European blocks.

It is therefore clear that it is not in the longer-term interest of India to drag its feet on the issue of Kashmir. It simply prolongs the agony and the inevitable will occur. What is sad is that it will create such a rancor that for decades there will be no real progress and the loss of life will continue. We fail to see the logic behind a failed tactical plan and continually ignoring the strategic and obvious goals for India. The fear that India will fall apart if Kashmir is allowed to "breakaway" and potentially create twenty two countries is just that. In any case no country can be held together for long on the basis of oppression by armed forces and India knows this from its own example. The example of East Pakistan is a sad one as well for Pakistan. We hope and pray that there is no resurgence if the Kashmir issue is not resolved. This is because the economic element in any uprising is a very important factor and every penny that India spends against the military struggle in Kashmir is the penny it does not have for the betterment of its people. Our final recommendations to Obama administration (as he indicated some interest in the issue during campaigning) is go for any of the solutions above; any decision is better than none.

8.6 Other Regions

There are problems galore throughout the world and we can spend several volumes the size of this book talking just about the foreign policy. We have purposely avoided analyzing in any real detail the wars in Iraq and Afghanistan for a simple reason – they are the result of a confused domestic policy and misinformation. The attacks of 2001 now known popularly as the 9/11 attacks baffled the leadership in ways difficult to describe. One thing is clear; the entire world was in sympathy with the United States and wanted to do whatever was possible to remedy the situation. Focusing on Afghanistan was the right thing, but we made serious tactical mistakes as we have been told. However, getting bogged down in Iraq was a serious blunder, for which we will pay a heavy price for years to come. There are other perennial items as well – today the sympathy for the United States has evaporated.

A word or two about Russia - the country is vast in area more than twice that of the United States but less than half the population of the

US. It has a vast stock pile of nuclear arsenal, oil and gas; and if it wants to, blocks anything from happening in the United Nations. The sanity of the leadership on both sides is to not perpetuate a rivalry that makes no sense. The longer term prognosis is that the Europeans will move closer to the Russians, unless Russia makes blunders. If the Russians can attract about fifty million well fed and highly educated immigrants from around the world in the next fifty years (and that is a big IF), they could seriously challenge the United States for the leadership of the *peaceful* World.

China has come a long way and threatens similarly to take over the United States but not as potently as Russia. The country is still under-developed in the deep country side and infra-structure. More importantly it is still far behind in high technology and is doing what the United States and Russia accomplished in the space race in the late sixties. Unless our current troubles paralyze us and we become very slow, the Chinese will take another forty years (not so much in GDP) to snatch that prize. I cannot forget the country of Indonesia. It is a sleeping giant and does not get involved so easily in world politics. It is however, the largest Muslim country closing in on the 250 million people mark and can play a crucial role in bringing the United States closer to the Muslim World. The good news is that Mr. Obama has spent a few days in that country as a child and may be welcome as one of their own – let's hope so.

Clearly the Obama administration will have its hands full on all the hot spots not just the two described in some detail. If we look at the continent of Africa, there are problems from Somalia to Chad, from Sudan to Zimbabwe. May be if we can stop the carnage in Congo, Obama will have already achieved more success than Georg Bush with this just one thorny civil war. If he could talk to Sudan regarding Darfur, and in terms of immediate results, if he could give Somalia's coastal problems a hand, it will help greatly in reversing the prestige of the United States. On a continental basis, Asia needs help, Africa needs help, Latin America needs help, and even Eastern Europe and Caucasus need help. The only place not mired in war alliances yet is the continent of Antarctica – let's pray it stays that way.

Given our resources the President will have to keep his eyes on the priorities on foreign policy chess board, keeping them pieces poised as winnable as possible and apply as steady a brain as possible. We end this chapter by wishing him good luck. As long as the man has lived he has engaged in wars. The only way out is to raise the conscious levels and try and try again.

CHAPTER IX
Religions and Their Influence

9.0 God and Bringing Islam and Christianity Together
This chapter is an attempt on my part to bring the two great religions together. First and the foremost thought on the question in anyone's mind might be: Is it really possible or are we asking for the impossible; it is as though I am asking of the coming back of Jesus. Is it possible for Obama to do anything in regards to bringing the two religions together? Is any progress possible? May be not – but I will still try to fictionalize my intense desire for them to come together. Let us ask a potent question: *Who is a believer?* The reason for asking this question is to reason a bit with the agnostic (who doubt or have no opinion) as well as those who genuinely do not believe in God but *more importantly* to reason with those who "believe". If the Christian(s) regard Muslims as non-believers, then perhaps it has to be refuted with data and a formidable argument. Similarly, if the Muslims accuse the Christians to have violated the fundamentals by shedding strict monotheism then that has to be understood as well – but are those things really important?

To me the most fundamental difference between the "believer" and others is that the believers believe in Life after death and the disbelievers do not. The belief in God Himself is more of an abstract concept in the unseen which really does not affect the human beings until someone talks about the "hereafter". Then Hell, Heaven, the day of resurrection, and the Justice by God is invoked. For Jews, Muslims, and many Christians then "God's moral and other laws" are invoked and we are told that by those laws we have to spend our daily lives – That's when all the differences begin to emerge and the followers of different religions are forced to disagree. They ask why they should obey a law that in their eyes is immoral, inconvenient, harsh, or simply oppressive. That is a crucial, practical and a mundane problem. The abstract belief in God, itself, from a practical point of view, might not be such an issue and all might agree that someone (or somehow) sustains life. The billions of Fish in the ocean are not fed by the humans (they are pretty new on the scene) and so on. While species may come and go, biological life will somehow be supported on the planet until the Sun swallows the Earth, or whatever. It is interesting to note that animals are not in the picture when it comes to obeying the moral laws. No one says that a lion has to make love to one lioness only, for life, and so on. It is left to nature and no religion interferes. The humans regard themselves as self-aware and responsible for the consequences of their action on a collective basis as the annihilation of the planetary life and the species is in their hands, including self-destruction.

So if we restrict the argument to ***belief in the hereafter***, both Christians and Muslims are believers. The basis of all other differences is in the application of the "law" which is then justified on an abstraction. We are not going to debate the issue of whether Jesus came to annul the law (hence eating of the pork and no circumcision etc.). That is an internal debate within Christianity. Both Muslims and Christians agree that each is entitled to their way of prayers and the morality of one is not to be imposed on the other. In practical terms, throughout the history of Islam, and countries pre-dominantly Muslim, the law does not forbid Christians from eating pork and predominantly Christian countries do not force Muslims to eat pork. Similarly, there is hardly any difference (except in sincere nuances) in human "interactive morality" from both.

9.1 Can God Do Anything?
An ordinary believer might ask: what kind of a question is that? When my children asked me that question thinking my answer will be a sure yes, they were surprised when I said NO! I asked them for the simplest definition of God in their mind. They said God is an entity that has dominion over everything. I stopped them and asked they reconfirm that. They said again; God has dominion over everything.

So that means He *cannot* throw us out of His dominion – that will be a paradox if He could. Thus if God has infinite dominion, it cannot become finite. He can let us die, change our faces, make us beg His mercy – but He cannot throw us out of His dominion. What else is it that He cannot do? Well it will be paradoxical again, if he could lie. He is the absolute truth – nothing but the truth. Therefore lying is neither in His definition, nor His nature and so on. If it creates a paradoxical situation, and it reduces God to our level, He is unable to do it - it cannot be done. It is essential to be absolutely clear about the fundamentals - what can and cannot be done. It is therefore important for Christians and Muslims, who together are better than fifty percent of the population of the Earth to come together and not quibble over fruitless debates which the non-believer then uses to lobby for "laws" which we all have to live with. Example: prostitution is legal in Nevada. It is the worst form of oppression against women. Would it be too much for both of them to combine forces against this oppression? Can God stop prostitution? Would that not be a paradox – having given us the capacity to determine right and wrong, good and bad, for us to make decisions and suffer the consequences and then take that right away? Could he not have made us all robots and so we could never disobey Him? Has he created principles which not only we are bound by, He is bound as well? If He changes any of those fundamental principles the Day of Judgment would have arrived?

What do the non-believers *believe in* after all? If the Christians and Muslims join forces, they don't have to accept defeat on the first line of defense and agree to a *complete* separation of religion and state, simply by being a majority of the electorate. Are we then not supposed to join forces to enjoin good and at least write to our leaders to forbid evil? The two joining forces will have some other "small" consequences – peace might simply break out by example. As a Muslim I will quote a few places where the Muslim book the Quran talks about Jesus and Christians in very sublime terms and defends Jesus' mother Mary (pronounced mar-yam in the original Arabic and Aramaic)

a. Please note that the Quran obviously refers to Muslims as believers but then goes on to tell them their relationship with the Christians (Chapter V verse 82) "And thou will find the nearest of them in *affection* to those who believe to be those who say: Lo! We are Christians. That is because there are among them priests and monks and because they are not proud". Please note the verse implies that in the service of God humility is required and Christian theological leaders have humility. Note that the word used in Arabic translated officially as "Christian" is "Nasara" The root word in Arabic for Nasara is Nasr meaning help. There appears to be some controversy even among the Christians on the origin of word "Christian" – first appears in translation of Greek (Roman?) origins – it is not an Aramaic or Arabic word.

b. Chapter XIX of the Quran is named "Mary" (Maryam) in her honor, the only woman to have received this honor. She is regarded as a pious Muslim, along with Jesus as the Prophet of Islam. The Quran describes in very sublime way the miracle of the virgin birth as when He (God) wants something He merely says "be" and it is (God is with word? Does He use the word "be" for creating anything? In Arabic the word is Kun).

c. Verses 30-33 of XIX: as a little child Jesus comes to the aid of her mother when she is being taunted (this miracle of Jesus is not in the bible) and "He spake: Lo! I am the slave of God. He hath given me the scripture, and hath appointed me a Prophet......... Peace on me the day I was born, and the day I die, and the day I shall be raised again".

d. Based upon my own family teachings, I regard Christians as brothers and have said so and written so elsewhere in my articles. I was taught that there are numerous schools of thought within Christianity and they are all worthy of respect in their theological scholarship. However, we the Muslims are closest to the philosophy of Saint Peter who thought and taught that in order for the gentiles to receive salvation, they must submit to the strict theological foundations of the Jewish law and obey the one and only one Almighty. Furthermore, that all human beings are equal in the eyes of that law. There is no difference between the Jew and the Gentile. Saint Peter was not supported politically by his own flock, in particular by Saint Paul. He suffered at the hands of the Romans greatly as well and was executed. This sadness is one of the few that has stuck with me since childhood. We impeded then our own evolution and continue to do so.

9.2 Sincere Democratic Forces or Trouble Makers?

While I like many of the tenants of democracy and the idea that people are the ultimate masters of their destiny and not a king or any other human sovereign, I am uneasy about human tendency to self-destruct. If democracy says that prostitution is legal, as in Nevada, and the "IRS" comes to collect taxes from the most oppressed, then democracy has failed us. If the so called sovereign States within these United States issue lottery, the worst form of regressive taxation on the poor, then this sovereignty is as oppressive as that of the worst kings of the past, regardless of the motives. Just because your motive is to spend the profits on schools does not allow you to perpetuate oppression, then democracy has failed us. Democracy has failed before (Greek and Roman times) and unless we figure out weaknesses and improve them, I am afraid that the Principle of Continuous Improvement will obliterate it the second time as well.

Those who sincerely want to see democracy flourish including the secularists, the atheists, and certainly Muslims and the Christians they must come to agree on certain boundary conditions on democracy itself. There must be a second order perturbation allowed which is significant enough in the equation that certain universal moral laws shall be institutionalized. If it turns out that under PCI, those moral perturbations are no longer applicable it must be debated by a people's congress/council which has some measure other than simply counting votes. Then a timeframe dictated be established in which each member of the electorate must be required to understand the issue.

If the polynomial of democracy ends at the first order (counting of votes), then lobbyists will run the institution of congress and corruption will permeate the system, and every Obama will run and fail against Washington D.C. until the entropy part of PCI begins to dominate and a decay of this country hastens. Those living in this country are almost all patriotic and do not want to see their country lose the leadership position it has on the planet and beyond. We have cognition that even the Pharaohs folded after three thousand years – so we could still have a long time of "greatness" of democracy ahead of us provided we have cognition of PCI.

9.3

Is the United States henceforth Muslim? You might think I am provocative at best and delusional at worst and this book is turning in to total fiction. But I remember forty years ago when those who would confess to being Muslim were barely a hundred thousand. Today that number is in the millions. Forty years is nothing in the history of nations. The process of becoming Muslim is *not* about turning on or off a switch. It is *not* about putting a gun to your head and forcing you to accept Islam as your religion (There is no compulsion - propaganda aside). It is about living next to a Muslim, working with a Muslim, arguing with a Muslim, beating up a Muslim, oppressing a bunch of Muslims, but ultimately falling in love with them; even, in the jails, the toughest of the convicts fall in love with Islam. It is to know that Muslims are fallible; it is to know that they are human beings, it is to know bits of Quran, It is to know that the Quran speaks fondly of Mary; it is to know that Islam is the only religion that accepts Jesus as part of their theology.

We are however, allowed to ask questions that might make some happy, others uncomfortable, but one thing is clear; the Muslims of America are different and the Christians of America are equally different. Both have left the motherlands to go beyond the partisan theology and inspired the motherlands to accept the leadership of the new world. President Jefferson had a copy of the Quran and understood a lot of it. He and other founding fathers never used the word Jesus or the Father in the Heaven (when penning down the constitution) but always the monotheistic representation by using the word God. *In my humble opinion Jefferson was indeed the first Muslim President of the United States.* He could have never acknowledged being a Muslim. Mr. Obama is not a Muslim and we accept that but America has made real progress. There will be a time when someone will openly proclaim to be a Muslim or a Mormon or whatever else and win the presidency, if he/she deserves it – that is a good thing in democracy and we must keep it that way.

The United States and its people have followed good examples from history regardless of the source. I mentioned this in my previous book under the chapter "The Quran and the United States". It is worth repeating one of the paragraphs. When Muhammad thought of the collection of taxes (mostly voluntary during his time), he sent several representatives to do so. One of these men, very honest, came back with collection divided in two parts. He said (and we are paraphrasing): O Prophet of God there is the part meant to have been given to the State and the other offered to me personally. Please refer to "The Prophet's Establishing A State..." by Dr. M. Hamidullah, Centre Culturel Islamique Series, Paris, France, No. 6. The Prophet mounted on the pulpit thereafter and corrected the acceptance of personal gifts in essence saying the gifts belong to the State and would not have been offered, if the collector was not an officer of the

State. Notice that when a President of the United Sates or First Lady, are offered personal gifts, they belong to the State. Domestic gifts must be logged by the White House Gift Unit and managed by one of several domestic agencies, while gifts from foreign officials are managed by the State Department. They are managed under the Foreign Gifts and Decorations Act, the Presidential Records Act, and subsequent amendments to both, and must be disclosed on the Standard Form 278 created under the Ethics in Government Act. Under the Code of Federal Regulations, these disclosures must identify the gifts and their value.

The example above is one from history and its manifestation in the United States, I am proud of. Now we are in deep economic crisis at the writing of this book and I have said that it is my sincere wish that some boundary conditions be imposed in the laws that are drafted for this great country. Let me go back to history, a bit of the story was narrated in chapter one, and mention a gentleman named Hakim-ibn-Hazm who has narrated an important question/answer session with Prophet Mohammad. His father was Hizam-ibn-Khuwaylid who was a merchant. He asked Prophet *Mohammed whether it was permissible for him to sell to a customer, goods that he has not yet bought or does not yet posses ("Short Selling" in the New York Temple?). Prophet Mohammed responded by saying NO. This might* make the individual who is already rich even richer but the nation on a longer term basis may face a larger crises. The gambling aspect has to be removed. Note that selling of stocks and bonds does not come under the same restrictions. Unfortunately our banking system is based upon a similar partly oppressive theory – that things will be necessarily more expensive/cheaper tomorrow than today (?). Hence there must be a determination of significant interest and not a sense of sharing of profit and loss. This creates inflation. But even more oppressive is the credit card interest rates; those are akin to plain old usury, another place where democracy needs PCI. Similarly, another look at options and futures trading will be wise. No one is arguing about turning off a switch but is it not unfair that the tax-payer at large has to bear the burden of greed of the folks trading in the temple of New York and must we ask Jesus to allow us to turn the tables. I will bet, that both Christian and Muslim theology does not allow any of this oppression.

9.4

The Jewish Fears

One of the problems that has not been solved in the last several thousand years is the Jewish fear that the rest of the planet is out to ensure their extinction. I for one would agree with Jewish people to a great degree given the satanic behavior of Hitler and so on. If it turns out that the Muslims and Christians can get together in the name of humanity, the next step will be to bring the "older brother" in the fold, and promise him that no attempt shall be made a) to proselytize Jews and b) the younger two brothers will raise their guns against those who believe in the collective punishment of the Jewish people. In fact I will go as far as to enshrine this in the United Nations Charter for *any* people. If the nations could agree to even a milder form of this type of charter, the specter of wars can be avoided significantly. In such a charter the majority of the population of a county could not be held responsible and thus an atomic bomb could not be dropped. These issues can only be raised in the cooler atmosphere of "absolute" objectivity. Here Mr. Obama can provide an objective pulpit if not much more. It might be good for him to take a few priests and rabbis and pray in a mosque and any other temples or churches with Muslims that will start the process of genuinely bringing us together.

Given all this respect and honor in Islamic Theology, do the Christians have a choice but to come closer to the Muslims? Here is the challenge to the American Christians. If you folks don't come closer to us American Muslims and jointly fight the non-believing trouble makers we will steal from you Jesus and all his disciples and everyone else we like – even Saint Nichols and no one will bring any gifts to you.

CHAPTER X
What's in it for Me

10.0 The Question

The reader may ask a relevant question as to why have I written this book, and what's in it for me? If I were to simply say nothing, the reader will simply not believe. So let me give a little explanation. Let us look to the scriptures. In the context of the Old Testament Prophets and Messengers of God, the Quran has something very profound to say: Chapter XXXVI Verses 20-21; "and there came from the uttermost part of the city a man running. He cried: O my people! Follow those who have been sent. *Follow those who ask of you no fee, and who are rightly guided*". I dare not declare myself to be a prophet or a messenger, because I am not, but I can follow in the footsteps of those prophets, in their teachings and behavior and ask nothing in return for the time and energy I have spent in writing this book. I can assure you that I am not wrongly guided either – this book is a proof of that. I began writing in earnest at the end of November 08 and I am done by January 1, 09. Two months without any help from anyone, not even anyone to type any part of the manuscript.

Look to the examples of Moses, Jesus and Mohammad. Moses was living just fine in the palaces of Pharaohs. There was no reason to upset the establishment. But he raised his voice against oppression for no worldly reward. Jesus in essence said that his kingdom is not about this world, and never asked for anything in return for himself even while turning the tables in Jerusalem. He could have asked for a million pieces of gold and they would have been happy to oblige. Mohammad was given every opportunity to settle for the gold and kingship which he refused every time; and merely told the followers that there is no difference among human beings and that, they are one in the application of God's law and His mercy. The determination of the level of piety is between the man and his God. I am referring to the Quran because in it every prophet is spoken of in the most sublime and respectful way never accusing anyone of any immoral acts, and excuses.

Let us talk a bit about President George Washington who led the continental army to victory over Britain in the revolutionary war. Following the end of war (1775-1783) he returned to private life *not* looking for anything, when he could have become a king, and did not even become President until 1789. He warned the nation against partisanship, sectarianism, and *getting involved in foreign wars – all the lessons we have forgotten.* It is clear from his life example that a great leader never looks to a reward from the nation. Now his face is on the dollar and I am already beginning to miss him. The dollar buys so little, far less than before, that we take out a higher denomination bill. In any case, without reading glasses the face is invisible. As a child, I read about the founder's of several nations, and discovered that in one way or the other, it was an example similar to those of the prophets mentioned above – asking for nothing.

Finally let us talk about someone who inspired me as a teenager, in 8th grade, in the uttermost part of the world, President John F. Kennedy. It wasn't until President Kennedy announced the plan to put a man on the moon in ten years that I seriously became interested in learning Physics. I was growing up with both parents dead and supported by my aunt. I never thought of receiving anything from anybody then, and I still don't. It was the pursuit of knowledge that brought me to this country. The United States was then a leader in the true sense, where the force of ideas was more powerful than the force of the atomic bomb. The country and its leader inspired an orphan growing up far away from this land. President Kennedy said and you know this by heart; "ask not what the country can do for you, ask what you can do for the country". It has been more than forty years and I still live by that sentence. So, if the nation accepts this book as a gift and I make nothing out of it, I am perfectly happy.

On a national basis we have a lot to gain or lose depending on how the leadership behaves going forward. The bad news is that our children and grand children could face trillions of dollars in debt burden and a currency so weak historians begin to talk about Germany before the war. Recently the clock has been turned back and most of the world has a bad feeling about this country. I would like to see the leadership to think of ways that in a poor country an orphan is inspired once again by the leadership in the United States. So Mr. Obama has some very high expectations from everyone in the United States and the World. The good news is that he was essentially raised as an orphan and learned to work hard in his childhood. The good news is that he seems to have a good start and appears to have gathered a reasonable team of experts. The good news is that the nation is willing to call it the "first day of the rest of our lives" and allow him to move ahead without rancor.

10.1 The Answer

So if there is something for me; it is that I would like to leave behind *our* progeny in a nation that is at least as good, as it was when I first landed in Philadelphia almost forty years ago and visited the Liberty Bell. The nation faced many problems then as well but it came out looking better than before. The war in Vietnam had fractionalized the country, and later the Water-Gate scandal badly demoralized it. However, the feelings of optimism and hope came back quickly, as they have at the start of the Obama Administration.

So if there is something for me it is this: It gives me a great deal of satisfaction that I have done my duty in telling the nation that it must realize that it cannot have a set of optional wars, a set of trillion dollar deficits, and then look for a tax-cut at the same time. The time of sacrifice is here and anyone who is unwilling to live on less than 2000 calories and 68 degree F warmth in winter is wasting money and any regulation anywhere in the nation must be fixed. The regulations must be changed so that all the frivolous lawsuits are discouraged and the judges and the court system comes down hard on civil court cases and punitive damages, and these cases will stand no chance of going anywhere. It is time for the government to start looking at ways to reduce fines in the court system on people who can least afford them and fix them based upon "justice" and not on what the insurance coverage provides for. It is time for the consumers to stop buying things they will use for a few days and then store it in their garages only to be thrown away for pennies in a sidewalk sale. It is time to move a bit down in square footage in cars and homes by cutting down on the fat - body, decadence, and show-off.

I would like to end the book with a historical warning and what the Principle of Continuous Improvement teaches me every day. If you are standing still, in effect you are falling behind and decaying in all walks of life. It is not true that if something works, leave it alone. The leaders of this country have recently hurt the nation more so than ever before; in the oval office, in the cold of Alaska, and in the stench of a bathroom. The new leaders starting with President Obama have a special duty towards the people of this country to right the wrongs and avoid those wrongs going forward. No one expects the leaders to be saints and there will be mistakes on a daily basis. But the decay of the nation will not be allowed and we expect that the leadership will continually improve in form and function on all fronts.